HOW TO STUDY YOUR BIBLE for kids

KAY ARTHUR
JANNA ARNDT

HARVEST HOUSE PUBLISHERS
Eugene, Oregon 97402

All Scripture quotations are taken from the New American Standard Bible®, © 1960, 1962, 1963, 1968, 1971, 1972, 1973, 1975, 1977, 1995 by The Lockman Foundation. Used by permission.

The word study material on pages 90-92 is from Spiros Zodhiates, ed., *The Complete Word Study Dictionary: New Testament,* ©1992 by AMG Publishers, Chattanooga, TN. Used by permission.

The concordance material on pages 81-82 is from *The New American Standard Exhaustive Concordance®,* ©1981 by The Lockman Foundation, La Habra, CA. Used by permission.

The dictionary material on page 94 is from W.E. Vine, *Vine's Expository Dictionary of Old & New Testament Words,* ©1997 by Thomas Nelson Publishers, Nashville, TN. Used by permission.

Illustrations by Steve Bjorkman

Cover by Left Coast Design, Portland, Oregon

Harvest House Publishers, Inc., is the exclusive licensee of the registered trademark DISCOVER 4 YOURSELF.

Discover 4 Yourself™ Bible Studies for Kids

How to Study Your Bible for Kids

Copyright © 2001 by Precept Ministries International
Published by Harvest House Publishers
Eugene, Oregon 97402
www.harvesthousepublishers.com

ISBN 0-7369-0362-3

Printed in the United States of America.

03 04 05 06 07 / ML / 10 9 8 7 6

To my husband, Jerry:
Thank you for all those long hours of designing our puzzles and mazes, for all your
prayers and encouragement. I couldn't do it without you!

I am so blessed to have a husband who loves his wife the way Christ loves
the church and is also the very best dad!

I love you with all my heart!

Janna
Psalm 78:4

To my precious granddaughters
Jesse, Abigail, Annie, and Alexandra:
These studies were written for you and other precious children like you,
so you can learn God's Word and walk in it all the days of your life.
"You, however, continue in the things you have learned and become convinced of,
knowing from whom you have learned [them]; and that from childhood you have known
the sacred writings which are able to give you the wisdom that leads to salvation
through faith which is in Christ Jesus" (2 Timothy 3:14-15).

I love you—"a bushel and a peck."

Mimi
Deuteronomy 4:9-10

Contents

The Mystery: How to Study the Bible for Yourself

Hi! Climb on up! This tree house is the home of "M and M Detectives"! I'm Max and this is my partner, Molly. We hear that you have a big mystery on your hands, and we're excited that you've asked us to help you solve this very important case. Oh, I almost forgot. This is Sam, the best detective beagle around. Sam is great at sniffing out clues and howling an alarm if we wander into any danger. But don't worry. I know we'll have some great adventures solving this mystery, but we shouldn't run into any danger.

Molly, why don't you get a file started on this case? Let's see…. Why don't we call this case "The Mystery of How to Study the Bible"? After all, that's what you're here for, isn't it? To learn how to study God's Word for yourself. This is really going to be exciting, learning how to study the Bible.

"M and M Detectives" use the inductive study method to get to the truths of the Bible. That word *inductive* means that you will investigate the Bible and discover *for yourself* what it means, instead of depending on what someone else says it means.

In order for a detective to get all the facts to solve his case, he has to have certain skills. That's what you will be doing each week as you go through our inductive detective training. You will learn the skills you need to know so that you can discover what the Bible says, understand what it means, and apply it to your life all on your own. Then, whatever happens, you'll be able to discover truth for yourself! Isn't that awesome?

We can't wait to get started because if you are ever going to really know God, have a relationship with Him, and experience His power in your life you need to understand what His Word says and live just like He says. We need to get on this case right away. Are you ready to join the "M and M Detectives" and help us get to the bottom of this awesome mystery? If so, there are a few things that every good Bible detective needs:

Things You'll Need
▼

NEW AMERICAN STANDARD
BIBLE (UPDATED EDITION—OR
PREFERABLY THE *NEW INDUCTIVE
STUDY BIBLE*, THE NISB)
PEN OR PENCIL
COLORED PENCILS
INDEX CARDS
A DICTIONARY
THIS WORKBOOK

Now we're ready to go!

1

Just the Facts

The Mystery of Observation, Interpretation, and Application

Before we learn how to discover truth for ourselves, we need to cover something every good inductive detective needs to do: staying in communication with "Central Headquarters." An inductive detective needs a heavenly cellular phone, so to speak, so he or she is always in touch with God. Or to put it another way, you need a satellite walkie-talkie. So as you search out truth, you keep talking to God and asking for His direction, His help. The Bible calls this *prayer!* So the very first thing that we need to do is to pray and ask God to direct and teach us by His Spirit so that we can understand all the wonderful things in His Word.

Why don't you pray before we go any further in our investigation and just say something like this to God:

> *God, I have my hand over my ear to let You know I need Your help. Show me truth, tell me what to do, and I'll believe You and do it. I ask this in the name of Your Son, Jesus Christ, who loves me, died for me, who sits at Your right hand, and is praying for me as I learn to study Your Word. Thank You, God. Thank You so much. Amen.*

Now let's look at the three steps to studying the Bible inductively: observation, interpretation, and application.
Read the words and say them aloud several times.

1. Observation

2. Interpretation

3. Application

1. Observation asks the question, WHAT does this say?

Good detectives are very observant. They ask a lot of questions. Getting the facts straight is very important to a detective. That's what observation is all about: getting the facts by asking the right questions. We call them the Who, What, When, Where, Why, and How questions or, to put it in inductive terms, the "5 W's and an H."

Here's a good way to remember what observation is, kind of like a code. Take your hands and make two circles like you are wearing glasses. Put them in front of your eyes, now move your hands away from your eyes toward your page six times—one for each of the 5 W's and an H. Each time you do this shout, "Who?" or "What?" or "When?" or "Where?" or "Why?" or "How?" Do it until you can say all six from memory. Every good detective needs to be able to ask these questions from memory.

(When you meet another inductive detective, this could be like a secret handshake!)

2. *Next comes interpretation. Interpretation asks the question, WHAT does this mean?*

A good detective first gets the facts and then figures out what they mean. Just remember: Observation is the key to unlocking the mystery of interpretation, so observation should always come before interpretation.

Try this to remember what interpretation is. Point to your brain with your finger and say, "Interpretation—what does this mean? Hmmmmm." (Remember, inductive detectives: Think things through. Then sort out the facts!)

3. *The third step is application. Application asks, HOW does the meaning of this truth, these facts, these commands and instructions in the Bible apply to me? What am I to believe? What am I to do?*

That means as you learn what God's truths are, you will make a choice whether you will believe what God says or not, and whether you will obey God and do what He says.

To help you remember what application is, take your hands and turn your head to the right to show you're going to believe what is right! Then turn your body that way and walk several steps to the right and say, "Application—believing and doing what God says is right." Practice this several times.

Now do observation, interpretation, and application until you can do them from memory. Teach this to someone else: your brother, sister, mom or dad, grandmother or grandfather.

Now that you have the facts, match each part of inductive study below by drawing a line from each part of inductive study with the correct question it asks. Then do the gesture that goes with it.

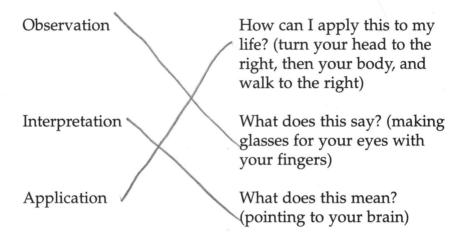

Observation

Interpretation

Application

How can I apply this to my life? (turn your head to the right, then your body, and walk to the right)

What does this say? (making glasses for your eyes with your fingers)

What does this mean? (pointing to your brain)

Sometimes a detective will get messages written in secret code. See if you can unscramble this secret coded message (your memory verse) to remind you why it's important to know God's Word.

In this message the first letter to each word is the last letter in the scrambled word. Unscramble the message and write it out on the lines, then read it aloud three times today. To discover which verses these are, read 2 Timothy 3 in your Bible and write the number of the matching verses in the blanks at the end.

__ __ __ __ __ __ __ __ __ __ __ __ __ __ __ __ __ __ __ __
l l A c r i p r u e t S s i n s p i d e r i

__ __ __ __ __ __ __ __ __ __ __ __ __ __ __ __ __ __ __
y b o d G n d a r o t i f b a e l p o r f

Realizing that the Pokémon and their clones are destroying each other, Ash tries to stop Mewtwo — but gets caught in the crossfire! Will Ash survive?

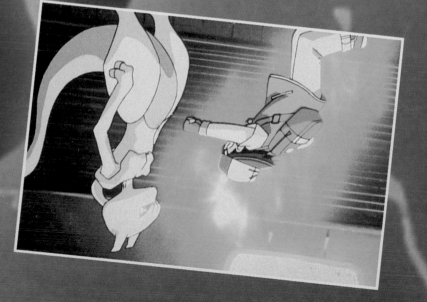

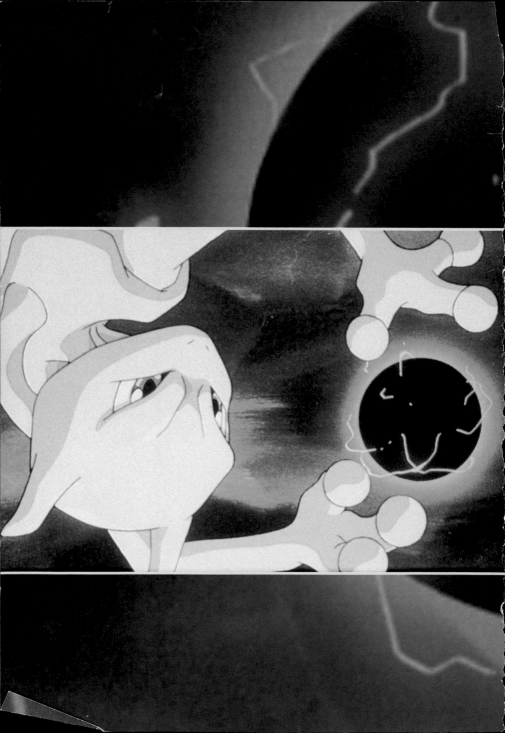

_ _ _ _ _ _ _ _ ,   _ _ _   _ _ _ _ _ _ _ _ ,
a h e n i c g t   o r f   e p o r o f r

_ _ _   _ _ _ _ _ _ _ _ _ ,   _ _ _
o r f   o e c t r r o n i c   o r f

_ _ _ _ _ _ _ _   _ _   _ _ _ _ _ _ _ _ _ _ _ ;
r a i n g n i t   n i   i g h t e o u s s e n s r

_ _   _ _ _ _   _ _ _   _ _ _   _ _   _ _ _
o s   h t a t   h e t   a n m   f o   o d G

_ _ _   _ _   _ _ _ _ _ _ _ ,
a y m   e b   d e q a u t e a

_ _ _ _ _ _ _ _   _ _ _   _ _ _ _ _
q u i p e p d e   o r f   v e r y e

_ _ _ _   _ _ _ _
o d o g   o r k w

2 Timothy 3: ____ - ____

Great detective work! Tomorrow we will look at our first case to help us solve the mystery of how to study the Bible. See you then!

The Mystery of Context

What Is Context?

Have you ever read a mystery or watched a detective story on television? If so, you know the police or the members of the investigative team always carefully examine the scene of the crime to see if they can find any clues. For instance, if some jewelry and money were stolen out of someone's bedroom, the investigators wouldn't just check out the bedroom. They would check out the whole house to see if they could find any clues, like a broken door or window or fingerprints in other rooms. That is context. Context is the setting in which something is found.

Context is a very important investigative procedure when you study the Bible. It's a combination of two words: *con* which means "with" and *text*. "Text" is what is written. So when you look for context in the Bible, you look at the verses surrounding the passage you are studying (like checking out every corner of the house as well as the bedroom). Then you also think about where the passage fits in the big picture of the Bible (like checking out the neighborhood or the city).

Context also includes:

- The place where something happens. (This is *geographical context*, such as Jerusalem instead of Los Angeles.)

- The time in history when an event happens. (This is *historical context*, such as the time before Jesus' birth or after His life and death.)

- The customs of a group of people. (This is *cultural context*, such as girls in Bible times did not wear blue jeans, and when the people ate dinner, they reclined on a couch rather than sitting at a table.)

Sometimes you can discover all these things from just the verses you're studying. But sometimes you have to study other passages of Scripture. It is always important to be on the lookout for "Commissioner Context"—he's the boss of the investigative agency that makes sure everything is interpreted correctly. He knows this important rule:

Scripture never contradicts Scripture.

In fact, Scripture is the best interpreter of Scripture. Context helps you discover what the Bible is saying.

Now how do we discover the context? We find context by observation. We begin by looking at the things that are obvious —the things that are the easiest to see. When a detective observes the scene of a crime, the first thing he looks for are the things that are right in front of his eyes.

In the Bible the three easiest things to see are always:

1. people (WHO?)

2. events (WHAT?)

3. places (WHERE?)

People are the easiest to see because they have names or go by I, you, he, she, we, or us.

Clue #1: WHO

WHO wrote it? To WHOM was it written? WHO is it about?

Clue #3: WHEN

WHEN did it happen or will it happen? WHERE did it happen, or WHERE was it said?

Clue #4: WHY

WHY was this book of the Bible written? WHY did God include it in the Bible? (Sometimes the author gives an exact reason for writing, and sometimes the WHY will be revealed by what is repeated, talked about the most, or the commands or instructions that are given. Look up John 20:31. This is an example of an author telling his reason for writing.)

Clue #2: WHAT

WHAT did they say? WHAT did they do? WHAT is the main topic?

Let's say you are going to put a puzzle together. Where do you start? What pieces of the puzzle do you look for first? The four corners, of course! Why? Because they are the easiest to see since there are only four of them (unless it is a round puzzle). You can pick out the corners right away because they have two straight sides. Look on page 15 and you will see the four corners of our puzzle that will give us the major clues we need to help solve the mystery of context.

Are you ready for your first big assignment? As a detective -in-training, you have been assigned to a major problem on the island of Crete. An important letter has been written that needs to be checked out. Everybody on Crete is not going to like what is said. Why? You'll see!

Turn to page 157 to your Observation Worksheets on Titus. An Observation Worksheet is a chapter of the Bible that you're going to search for information to get the facts, just the facts. It's pure truth!

You need to discover WHO wrote this letter and to WHOM is was written. Time is short, but let's get the main facts, go for the obvious by reading all of the first chapter of Titus.

1. Mark every reference to the author of the book (WHO) in a special way. Color these references blue.

2. Mark every reference to the recipient (the WHOM it was written to) by coloring it orange.

And don't forget to make sure you mark the pronouns that refer to the author and to the recipient each in the right color. The author will use the pronouns *I* or *we*, or *us*. The pronouns for the recipient (the one to whom the letter is written) will be *you* or *yourself*.

What's a pronoun? Check out the "Detective Clue Box" that follows:

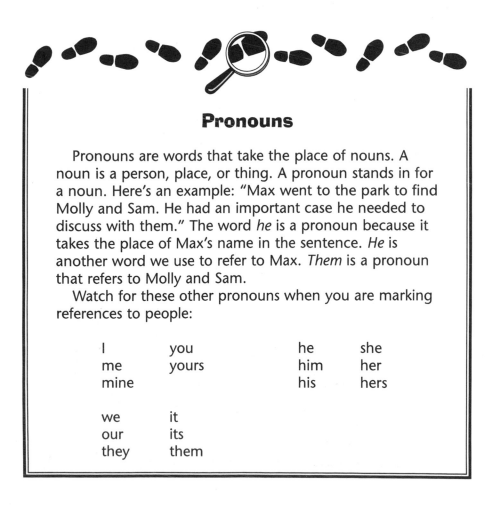

Pronouns

Pronouns are words that take the place of nouns. A noun is a person, place, or thing. A pronoun stands in for a noun. Here's an example: "Max went to the park to find Molly and Sam. He had an important case he needed to discuss with them." The word *he* is a pronoun because it takes the place of Max's name in the sentence. *He* is another word we use to refer to Max. *Them* is a pronoun that refers to Molly and Sam.

Watch for these other pronouns when you are marking references to people:

I	you	he	she
me	yours	him	her
mine		his	hers
we	it		
our	its		
they	them		

Also pay attention to WHOM the author is writing. We call this the recipient or recipients (if it's more than one person). Help Max by filling in your answers in the blanks below.

Clue #1:

WHO wrote the book? Titus 1:1 _____

To WHOM did he write? Titus 1:4 _____

Now here's a whopper of an assignment but a very important one.

WHOM is he writing about in chapter 1?

Titus 1:5: e __ __ __ __ s

and Titus 1:10: r __ __ __ __ __ __ __ __ s m __ __

Great investigation! Don't forget to practice your memory verse. A good detective has to develop his memory. To do that he says something out loud three times in a row. He does this in the morning, at noon, and at night before he drops into bed. (By the way, did you figure out that your memory verse is 2 Timothy 3:16-17?)

Learn to Ask the 5 W's and an H

There's a big problem on the island of Crete in the Mediterranean Sea (check out the map on the next page). Rebellious men are teaching some things they shouldn't be teaching. So we need to dig out information on the situation.

Molly and Max want to develop your observation skills by
having you read a letter telling about the situation. They want
you to do this because detectives need to have good interrogation skills to get the facts needed to solve their cases. When
you interrogate someone, you can learn so much by asking
WHO, WHAT, WHERE, WHEN, WHY, and HOW.

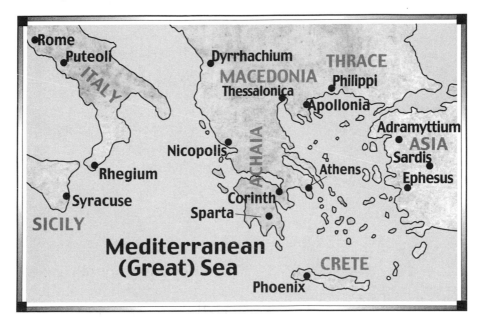

1. Asking WHO helps you find out:
    WHO wrote this?
    To WHOM was it written?
    WHO do we read about in this section of Scripture?
    WHO said this or did that?

2. WHAT helps you understand:
    WHAT is the author talking about?
    WHAT are the main things that happen?

3. WHERE helps you learn:
    WHERE did this happen?
    WHERE did they go?
    WHERE was this said?

When we discover a "where" we double underline the "<u>where</u>" in green.

4. WHEN tells us about time, and we mark it with a green clock like this: 🕐
    WHEN tells us:
    WHEN did this event happen or WHEN will it happen?
    WHEN did the main characters do something?
        This helps us follow the order of events, which is so important in investigative work.

This is why detectives are always asking people about when something happened or where they were. Time and place are critical when you are getting the facts.

5. WHY asks questions like:
    WHY did he say that?
    WHY did this happen?
    WHY did they go there?

6. HOW lets you figure out things like:
    HOW is this to be done?
    HOW did people know something had happened?

Now examine the evidence by turning to your Observation Worksheets on Titus on page 157. You have already colored the references to the author and to the recipient. Now look at those markings and ask yourself the 5 W's and an H! Let's do it for practice.

Read Titus 1.

Titus 1:1 WHO wrote the letter?

_____Paul_____

This is review. (See if you can remember his name.)

Titus 1:1 WHAT was Paul?

_____bond servant_____ of God and

_____ of Jesus Christ

Titus 1:4 To WHOM was Paul writing?

_____Titus_____

Titus 1:4 WHAT did Paul and Titus share?

a common _____Faith_____

Titus 1:5 WHERE did Paul leave Titus?

_____Crete_____

Titus 1:5 WHY did Paul leave him there?

to set _____

to_____

Titus 1:5 WHEN did Paul write this?

after he left _____

Character Profiles

Titus 1:6-9 is a list showing us WHAT kind of men Titus was to choose as elders. Which brings us to another step as an inductive detective: getting a profile on our main characters. List everything the Bible text tells you about these people. Do this for the author, the recipients, and other people who are mentioned. We're going to do it for the elders. By the way, what is the synonym used for *elders* in 1:7?

o _verses_ r

Character Profile #1

Fill in the blanks below to complete the list on choosing elders.

They must be above _reproach_,

husband of _one_ _wife_,

having children _who_ _believe_,

not accused of _dissipation_ or _rebellion_.

He must be above reproach as _God_ _steward_,

not _quick_-_tempered_, not quick-_tempered_,

not addicted to _wine_, not _pugnacious_,

not fond of _sordid_ _gain_.

He must be _hospitable_, loving what is _God_, _sensible_, _just_, _devout_,

self-_controled_, holding fast the _faithful_ _word_.

He will be able to _exhort_ in _sound_

__doctrine__ and to __refute__ those

who __contra dict__.

Character Profile #2

Titus 1:10 WHO else did Paul write about besides the elders?

rebelliuos, empty talkers and deceivers.

Titus 1:11 WHY must they be silenced?

_____

_____

_____

Titus 1:13 WHAT was Titus to do to them?

_____

Titus 1:13 WHY?

_____

Titus 1:16 WHAT do the rebellious profess to know?

_____

Titus 1:16 HOW can you spot these rebellious, deceiving men? HOW do they deny God?

_____

Titus 1:16 WHAT are they?

    a. d _____

    b. d _____

    c. w _____ for any _____ _____

These are the kind of men that detectives need to watch out for! Detectives also need a good memory. Being able to recall the facts is a must, so make sure you can remember this profile on rebellious men by describing them to another person.

Wow! Look at all the evidence you gathered! Molly and Max are thrilled with all the groundwork you have laid for our case. And Sam is standing on his hind legs howlin' and pawin' the air!

By the way, did you find out why some people in Crete wouldn't like Paul's letter? What did one of their own prophets (Titus 1:12) say about the Cretans?

They are always _____, _____

_____, _____ _____.

Track Them Down, Sam!

Sam is howlin'! (We call it beaglin' because that's what beagles do.) They don't yap—they howl when they catch the scent! Sam's so excited because he loves sniffing out clues. You better put him on a leash or you'll lose him! So hook him to his leash and head to your Observation Worksheet on Titus 2 on page 158. But don't forget to get out your heavenly cell phone. Talk before you walk. In other words, pray first before you and Sam hit the trail.

Read Titus 2 and let Sam lead you as you search for clues to solve the crossword puzzle that follows.

There are several groups of people mentioned in Titus 2 that you need to hunt down and instruct so they aren't led astray by those rebellious men. Sam will lead you to the people. First mark every reference to Titus in chapter 2 (like you did in chapter 1); then follow the puzzle path.

Across

1. Titus 2:1 WHAT are you to speak? Things fitting for sound _____

4. Titus 2:3 WHO are to be reverent in their behavior?
_____

5. Titus 2:4 WHO are the older women to encourage?
_____

6. Titus 2:4 WHAT are the older women to encourage the younger women to do?
to _____their husbands and children

7. Titus 2:5 WHY are the younger women to be sensible, pure, workers at home, kind, and subject to their own husbands? so that the _____ of God will not be dishonored

9. Titus 2:7 WHAT is Titus to be an example of?
good _____

11. Titus 2:10 WHY are they to do these things?
to _____ the doctrine of God our Savior

Down

2. Titus 2:2 WHO is Paul telling to be temperate?
_____

3. Titus 2:2 WHAT are the older men to be sound in?
sound in _____, in love, in perseverance

8. Titus 2:6 WHO is to be sensible?
_____

10. Titus 2:9 WHO are to be subject to their masters?
_____

12. Titus 2:11 WHAT did the grace of God bring to all men?
_____

13. Titus 2:13 WHO is going to appear from heaven, whose appearing is our blessed hope?
_____   _____

14. Titus 2:15 WHAT is Titus to do with all authority?
speak, exhort, and _____

Let's Close the Case

We have one more chapter in Titus to investigate before we can wrap up our first case, "The Case of Titus and the Cretans." Are you ready for a little more legwork? Then turn to page 159 and read Titus 3. Help us crack this case by interrogating the text. Begin by marking every reference to Paul and Titus (like you did in chapters 1 and 2).

In Titus 3:1-2 Paul is talking to Titus. WHO are the "them"? Get the facts straight. Check whether they are the rebellious men or the Christians at Crete. To do this, remember Commissioner Context. He would tell you to look at WHO Paul was talking to last and about WHOM. The "them" are the _____.

WHAT is Paul doing when he gives Titus this list of things to do in verses 1 and 2?

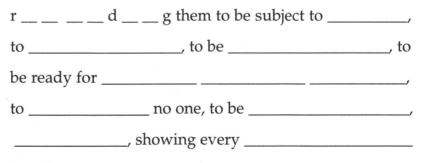

r __ __ __ __ d __ __ g them to be subject to _____,

to _____, to be _____, to

be ready for _____ _____ _____,

to _____ no one, to be _____,

_____, showing every _____

for all men

Hey, this would be a good time for a little application, wouldn't it? Ask yourself how you measure up to Paul's list. If 1 is the lowest score and 10 is the highest, what would you give yourself on each one of the things on the list Paul gave to Titus? Go back to the words you just filled in and put down the number that you rate yourself above each thing the Cretan Christians are to be.

Now let's get back to our interrogation.

Titus 3:5 WHAT did God do for mankind?

_____

Titus 3:5 HOW did He save us?

    a.   Because of our deeds? ___ Yes ___ No

    b.   According to His _____

Titus 3:7 HOW were we justified? (*Justified* means God's not going to hold our sins against us. He's going to give us Jesus' righteousness, pronounce us righteous, and put us in His family.)

_____

Titus 3:8 WHAT are the things we are to do, to engage in, if we believe in God?

_____

Titus 3:12 WHERE is Paul?

_____

Titus 3:12 WHAT does Paul want Titus to do?

_____

Titus 3:14 WHY are the people to engage in good deeds and meet needs?

_____

Titus 3:15 WHOM are they to greet?

_____

Wow! What a case! Your first one as an inductive detective!

You've learned two very important tools: context, and the 5 W's and an H to help you study the Bible.

Before we stamp our file case closed this week, find a grown-up or a friend and say your memory verse to that person.

> *All Scripture is inspired by God and profitable for teaching, for reproof, for correction, for training in righteousness; so that the man of God may be adequate, equipped for every good work.*
>
>   —2 Timothy 3:16-17

2

Get All the Facts: Observe, Observe, Observe

Sam is wagging his tail. He is sooooo glad to see you back at the tree house. We have another assignment for you since you aced the last one. Are you ready to gather more facts? If so, let's get started searching out key words, lists, contrasts, and terms of conclusion.

Wow! That sounds awesome, doesn't it? It is! Let's go.

Anonymous Notes

"Whoa, wait a minute, Sam!"

"Molly, take a look in that bush over by the tree. Do you see that piece of folded-up paper that Sam is trying to get?"

"Good sniffin', Sam."

"I'll get it," Molly said as she stood on tiptoe to reach it. As Molly unfolded the paper, you could see and hear her disappointment. "There's nothing on it, Max. It's totally blank."

"Hmmmm. There has to be more to it than that. I mean, we both know Sam wouldn't be having such a fit over a blank piece of paper. He's the best detective dog around. Let's take a closer look. Maybe there's a message written in invisible ink.

Let's head to my house and give this paper the invisible ink test."

"Hey, Mom," Max called out as he burst into the kitchen. "Sam found a clue that may be written in invisible ink, and we need some red or purple grape juice in order to check it out. Do we have any that Molly and I could use?"

"Sure, Max, I just went to the store. Look in the refrigerator on the top shelf," Max's mom said as she peeled the potatoes.

"Okay, Molly, you get the grape juice and I'll go find a paintbrush."

In three minutes Max was back in the kitchen. "I found one, Molly. Why don't you paint over the paper? I can hardly wait to see if anything is there!"

Molly and Max looked at the paper intently as Molly dipped the paintbrush into the grape juice and started painting over the paper.

"Oh, Max," Molly squealed, "look! Isn't this awesome?"

"Wow, look at that! Sam, ol' boy, you've done it again!"

There it was, as clear as ink!

Remind them to be subject to rulers, to authorities, to be obedient, to be ready for every good deed—Titus 3:1.

Sam thumped his tail on the floor and cocked his head. He was a doggone good detective!

"Hey, Molly, this verse has a key word in it, so our detectives-in-training need to memorize it. Let's have them write it out on an index card and practice saying it aloud three times every day this week."

Okay, inductive detectives-in-training, memorize your verse and then we'll teach you how to make invisible ink.

How to Make Invisible Ink and Decode Messages

You'll need the following items to go inside your detective's kit to make invisible ink or decode it.

baking soda
water
red or purple grape juice
cotton swabs
white paper
a paintbrush (like a watercolor paintbrush)

To make your invisible ink:
1. Place 1 teaspoon of baking soda in a small container or cup.
2. Pour in 1-2 tablespoons of water and mix well.
3. Take a cotton swab and dip it in the cup and write your message on a piece of white paper. Your message will be Titus 3:1.
4. Let your message dry completely. You can use a hair dryer to shorten the drying time, but ask your mom or a grown-up first. Don't put the hair dryer too close to the paper.
5. To make your message appear, pour some grape juice in a cup. Take your paintbrush, dip it in the cup of juice, and paint over the secret message. It will become visible!

Now that you know how to write invisible messages, let's continue our training by looking at another important skill that every good detective needs to know how to do: making lists.

Flip Open Your Notebooks

Have you ever noticed on television how the detective pulls out a notebook to take notes while he is at the scene of the crime? The detective will make a list of all the clues that he observes to help him solve his case.

Making lists is also very important to inductive Bible detectives because it helps them gather all the facts that are given about a certain word, subject, place, or event.

You made a list last week when you did a character profile on the elders. Remember, we said that you would also do this for the author, recipients, and other people mentioned. When you make a list, see if the facts in the list will answer the 5W's and an H questions.

Let's get some more practice learning how to use this very important tool by going back to the island of Crete and to our letter on page 157. Now pull out your detective notebooks and get the facts by doing a character profile on both Paul and Titus by making a list. Look at every place where you marked *Paul* or *Titus* and then list what you learn about each one of them below.

Paul

Titus 1:1 a _____ of _____

Titus 1:1 and an_____of J_____ C_____

Titus 1:3 entrusted with the

P__ __ __ __ __ __ __ __ __ __n

of the W ___ ___ d

Titus 1:5 left T_____ in _____

Titus 3:12 will send _____ or

_____ to Titus

Titus 3:12 will spend the w_____ at _____

Titus

Titus 1:4 Paul's t_____ c_____ in a

_____ _____

Titus 1:5 Titus is in _____.

Great descriptions! Flip your notebook closed, and we'll meet you back at the tree house tomorrow.

New Evidence

Before we open our files, get out that "heavenly cell phone"—your walkie-talkie! Remember, don't walk before you talk to God. You need His help in everything! Ask God by the power of the Holy Spirit to help you discover truth and find out which of those words in Titus 3:1 are key words.

One important tool in helping us gather new evidence by observation is identifying *key words*. Key words are words that pop up more than once. They are called key words because they unlock the meaning of the chapter or book you are studying and give you clues about what is most important in a passage of Scripture. Key words are important words that answer the 5 W's and an H. They tell you Who, What, When, Where, Why, or How.

Once you discover a key word, you should mark it in a special way using a special color or symbol so you can immediately spot it in the Scriptures. We'll show you how in just a minute.

When you mark a key word, you also need to mark any other words that mean the same thing, like pronouns or synonyms. We learned what pronouns were last week when we marked *Paul* and *Titus*. Look at the "Detective Clue Box" to learn about synonyms.

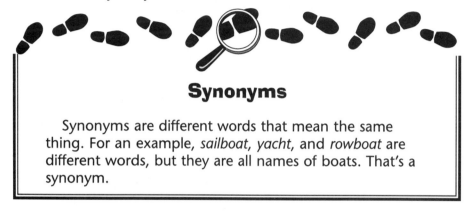

Synonyms

Synonyms are different words that mean the same thing. For an example, *sailboat*, *yacht*, and *rowboat* are different words, but they are all names of boats. That's a synonym.

So as you mark key words, always be on the lookout for any pronouns or synonyms that go with your key word and mark them in the same way.

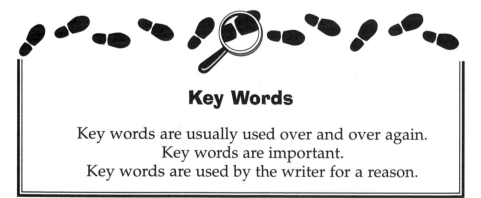

Key Words

Key words are usually used over and over again.
Key words are important.
Key words are used by the writer for a reason.

Are your ready to gather the evidence? Turn to page 157 of your Observation Worksheets on Titus. Read all three chapters of Titus and mark the following key words:

 deeds (green feet)   doctrine (color it pink and box it in blue)

By the way, a detective is always looking for any clues that tell him WHEN or WHERE, so mark any references to WHEN by drawing a green clock like this:  and mark WHERE by double underlining in green the words that tell you where.

Day Three

Taking Notes

As we said before, good inductive detectives are always very thorough in their observation. They pay close attention to everything that is said. And they constantly take notes. *Deeds* and *doctrine* are important key words. When you mark key words, you need to make a list of everything you learn from the use of that word. See if it tells you Who, What, When, Where, Why, or How.

Let's begin by looking at *doctrine* and see what we can learn from marking it. But before you do, make sure you've talked to the Lord. Then look at the "Detective Clue Box" for the meanings of *doctrine, sound,* and *deeds.*

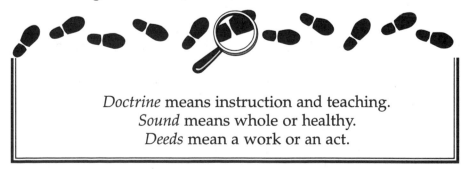

Doctrine means instruction and teaching.
Sound means whole or healthy.
Deeds mean a work or an act.

Now get out your notebook and turn to page 157. Make a list by writing down each fact that you observe from marking *doctrine* on your Observation Worksheets.

Doctrine

Titus 1:9-10 exhort in _____ doctrine

   a. WHO is to exhort? _____

   b. WHY? Because of the many r_____ m____

Titus 2:1 speak the things fitting for _____ _____

   WHO is to speak? _____

Titus 2:7 _____ in doctrine

   WHO is being spoken to? _____

Titus 2:10 _____ the doctrine of _____

   WHO is told to do this? (see verse 9) b_____

HOW do they adorn the doctrine? To adorn it means to display it, show it like it really is. Read verses 9 and 10 and list at least two ways to adorn the doctrine.

_____

_____

Good observations, inductive detectives! We'll practice this skill again tomorrow. But before you go, let's do a little application with what we learned. Do you tell other people that you believe that Jesus Christ is the Son of God, God in the flesh, the One we should believe, obey, and follow? This is doctrine. How do you adorn that? How do you live that shows you really believe?

_____

_____

Do you pilfer (that means steal), or are you absolutely honest? Are you always arguing, or do you keep your tongue under control? Underline which one describes you most of the time.

Examine the Clues

Remember the message that Sam discovered that had a key word in it? Can you say it from memory? And WHAT is the key word?

d __ __ __ s

Today we want to learn all we can about our key word *deeds*. Turn to page 157 and look for each place in Titus that you marked your key word *deeds*. Then make a list on each fact that you see from looking at *deeds*.

Deeds

Titus 1:16 by their deeds *they   deny   him*

WHO denies God by their deeds? _____

Titus 1:16 w*orthless*_ for any _*good*___ deed

WHO is this? _____

Titus 2:7   show yourself to be *an   example*

Titus 2:14 Christ redeemed us from *lawles deed*.

Titus 2:14 We are to be z*ealous*_____ for *good*
deeds.

Titus 3:1 Be ready for *every good deed*.

Titus 3:5 He saved us not on the *basis of deed*

Titus 3:8 Those who believe God are to *~~be careful~~ engage*
in *good*_____ *deed*_____.

Titus 3:14 People can *learn* to engage in *good*
deeds to *meet*_____ *pressing*
needs.

Now, inductive detectives, let's look at why it's important to observe key words. Remember what we learned about key words? They unlock the meaning of the chapter or book you're studying. Let's find out how they unlock the meaning for us.

In an investigation a detective looks at clues to help him understand why a crime was committed. When we study the Bible, key words are our clues that tell us why the author is writing the chapter or book.

Key words show us the subjects. When a word is repeated over and over, it is showing us the subject that the author wants to cover in his writing. Another word for the subject is the theme—what something is about. Seeing a subject repeated shows us the theme of the chapter and sometimes of the book in the Bible we are studying.

Remember:

key words

↓

show us (reveal)

↓

subjects (themes)

Now that you know how to discover the theme of each chapter of Titus, let's practice. Molly and Max have given you the theme to the book of Titus on the next page. They have also given you the theme for each chapter in Titus. But guess what? Sam rolled all over the pieces of paper and now they are all mixed up.

"Saaaaam, why did you do that? It's the doghouse, not the tree house for you!"

Why don't you return to the island of Crete on page 157 and look at each chapter. Match the themes with the chapters in the book of Titus by drawing a line to connect the right theme to the right chapter.

Book Theme: Speak Sound Doctrine, Engage in Good Deeds

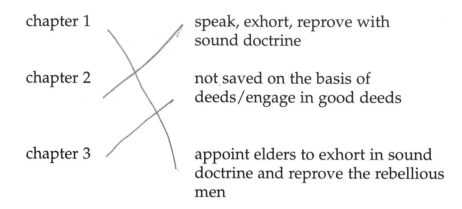

chapter 1   speak, exhort, reprove with
                             sound doctrine

chapter 2   not saved on the basis of
                             deeds/engage in good deeds

chapter 3   appoint elders to exhort in sound
                             doctrine and reprove the rebellious
                             men

Now that we have made our observations, we know that Paul's motive in writing Titus was

- to exhort him to speak sound doctrine

- to remind the people to do good deeds

Let's apply what we've learned.

Did you know that when you learn how to study your Bible inductively you are learning sound doctrine?

Do you believe what God says is true? __✓__ Yes ___ No

Then do you have sound doctrine? __✓__ Yes ___ No

Now take another look at 2 Timothy 3:16 (your verse from Week One) and then look at the "Detective Clue Box" on the next page.

Reproof means telling someone that
he is doing something wrong.
Correction means bringing back (restoring) to the right way.
Training in righteousness means instructing and correcting so that
we can be made right and have a right relationship with God.

When you study the Bible and you see that you are doing something wrong, do you change that wrong behavior? An example is where we discovered in Titus 2:9-10 about Paul urging the bondslaves to be subject to their masters.

Are you subject to your master? ___ Yes ___ No

WHO is your master?

_____

If you see that you are not obeying your mom and dad (your masters) WHAT do you do? Do you continue to do what you want, or do you let God's Word reprove, correct, and train you by obeying what He says?

_____

WHO is your master at school?

_____

Do you submit to your teacher's authority by being well pleasing and not argumentative? ✓ Yes ___ No

Do you show your teacher respect? Do you raise your hand to speak, and do you speak kindly? ✓ Yes ___ No

Do you argue or talk back to your teacher? ___ Yes ⟋ No

Do you obey those who are in authority over you (unless, of course, they would tell you or ask you to do something that God says is wrong)? ___ Yes ⟋ No

Thinking about HOW you treat those whom God has placed in authority over you shows you if your actions line up with God's Word.

If your actions don't line up with God's Word, ask God to show you how to do the right thing. Then do it! Remember, application is a choice that you make.

Now let's look at deeds. WHAT good deeds do you do? These might include helping neighbors by feeding their dogs while they are on vacation, using your allowance to buy a needy person something to wear, or being a friend to someone who doesn't have a friend.

Name two ways you engage in good deeds.

1. _____

2. _____

Molly and Max are so proud of you for your hard work in becoming an inductive detective and for applying what you've learned! And Sam is wagging his tail!

More Pieces to the Puzzle: Contrasts and Conclusions

Today we'll take a look at the two remaining skills in this case: *contrasts* and *terms of conclusion.*

Contrasts show how things are different or opposite, such as good and bad, black and white, day and night.

The Bible uses many contrasts, such as light and darkness, truth and lie, and life and death to help us examine what is being said. When we discover a contrast, we need to do further investigation and see what truth is being shown using these two different things or two different thoughts. Before we look at contrasts, did you remember to call on your heavenly Father for His wisdom and insight?

Now look at Titus 1:5-10 on page 157. Do you see the contrast between the elders (good men) and the rebellious men (bad men) who are empty talkers and deceivers?

And in Titus 3:5 WHAT contrast do you see? We are

saved not by deeds but by ___God___ ___mercy___ (WHAT)?

Deeds are contrasted with ___mercy___.

Read Acts 26:18 below and find the contrasts. Write them on the lines below.

> *...to open their eyes so that they may turn from darkness to light and from the dominion of Satan to God, that they may receive forgiveness of sins and an inheritance among those who have been sanctified by faith in Me.*

1. _____

2. _____

Read John 3:19 on the next page, find the contrast, and write it on the line.

"This is the judgment, that the Light has come into the world, and men loved the darkness rather than the Light, for their deeds were evil."

_____

Now let's investigate terms of conclusion. Terms of conclusion use words such as *therefore, for, so that,* and *for this reason* to show that a conclusion is being made or a result is being stated.

Just remember: Whenever you see a *therefore* in the Bible, look and see WHAT it is there for. Mark *therefore* with three red dots like this:

Since there is no term of conclusion in Titus, let's go to 1 Peter 1:25–2:2. It's printed out below. Read it and mark every reference to the Word (draw it blue like this and color it green).

"But the word of the Lord endures forever." And this is the word which was preached to you. Therefore, putting aside all malice and all deceit and hypocrisy and envy and all slander, like newborn babies, long for the pure milk of the word, so that by it you may grow in respect to salvation.

Sam is chomping at the leash. He's ready to sniff out the clue.

WHAT is the term of conclusion clue that Sam sees in 1 Peter 1:25–2:2? _____ Now answer this question:

WHAT is it there for? WHAT do you learn about the Word?

_____

_____

_____

WHAT will be the result?

_____

HOW does this apply to you? WHAT do you need to put away?

_malace_____

_____

_____

And then WHAT do you need to do—WHAT are you to long for?

_____

(By the way, that's how you get sound doctrine!)

As we close this case, see if you can write your memory verse in the blanks below without looking at your index card.

"_Remind_ them to be _subject_ to _rulers_, to _authorities_, to be _obedient_, to be _ready_ for every _good_ _deed_" —Titus 3:1.

You did a great job cracking this case! See you next week.

3

A New Adventure

Molly and Max are ready to help you with your next case as we move from skills that help us observe what the Bible says to skills that will help us understand what the Bible means (interpretation). Do your remember your gesture for interpretation? Let's practice it one more time. Where are you going to point that finger? That's right—to your head, because once you see what God's Word says, then you need to make sure you understand what it means.

Once a detective gathers all the facts, he has to figure out what the facts tell him, what they mean. It's the same with inductive detectives. First you observe, observe, observe. You get all the facts. Then you look for the plain meaning of it all. God means what He says and says what He means. Sometimes God will use figures of speech to make His point or teach a truth. Otherwise, He is going to speak in just plain words— and they mean what they mean. Remember, God wants you to understand Him, so He's not going to hide truth from you.

If you have questions about a Scripture or the meaning still doesn't seem clear or make sense, then like a good detective, you need to check out several other things. Let's look at them one by one.

1. *Check the context.* Remember "Commissioner Context," the boss of the investigative agency that makes sure everything

is interpreted correctly? He is known as "Commissioner Context" for a reason. A commissioner is a person in charge of some department or government bureau. "Commissioner Context" is in charge of context. The context (the setting in which something is found) is the boss (it rules) in interpreting Scripture. When you ask what a verse means, you need to be looking at:

a) the surrounding verses of Scripture

b) the book it is found in

c) how it fits into the whole Word of God

A good inductive detective will always ask the following questions:

- "Does what I think this means fit in with the theme, the purpose, and the structure of the book it is found in?"

- "Does it fit with other Scripture about the same subject, or is there an obvious difference?"

- "Am I considering the historical and cultural context in what is being said?"

2. Always look at the whole Bible. As you continue to study God's Word with us, doing the Discover 4 Yourself series and then the Precept Upon Precept Bible studies, you will become familiar with all that the Bible teaches book by book. Then you will know if what someone is teaching you fits into what the Bible says, or if it has been taken out of context. You will also know if some other Bible passages were overlooked that would have led to a clearer or fuller understanding. That's why it's important to be an inductive Bible detective so you will know God's Word for yourself and can protect yourself against wrong doctrine. You remember, don't you, what doctrine is? We are sooooo proud of you!

3. *Remember, Scripture never contradicts Scripture.* All Scripture is inspired by God; it is God-breathed, so it will never contradict itself. In fact, Scripture is the best interpreter of Scripture. If two or more truths taught in God's Word seem to conflict with each other and you cannot figure it out, remember that you are human and don't always understand God's mind. You have to decide to believe God even if you can't fully understand the passage at that moment. You know that God doesn't contradict Himself, and you have to trust Him and wait for Him to explain it. Nobody knows everything at once! And there is always more to learn, to discover for yourself.

4. *Don't base what you believe on an obscure passage.* Obscure means that it is not clearly understood. Sometimes people take a verse that is difficult to understand out of context and use it to contradict what is clearly explained in other passages. That is when they get into trouble! Some detectives have done that and messed up a whole case. They refused to look at the obvious and instead believed something that was not clear. Some passages are hard to understand even when you apply all the rules of interpretation. Passages that are not clearly understood should not be used to establish your doctrine, your beliefs.

Now that we know how to interpret let's look at our next case.

Figures of Speech: Parables, Symbols, Metaphors, and Similes

This next case is quite a mouthful! Let's get the facts first about *figures of speech*. What is a figure of speech? A figure of speech is a word, a phrase, or an expression that is used in a creative way, where words are not taken literally.

For example, Max's mom often uses the phrase "Hot spit!" that she used as a teenager, which meant something was really cool. "Really cool" does not mean that something is cool or cold to the touch, but that it's awesome or really neat. And "neat" doesn't mean orderly, like in a row or not messed up. It just means something is "in"—something everybody thinks is cool, or as Max's mom would say, "Hot spit!" "Hot spit," "cool," "neat," and "in" are all used figuratively in these sentences. They are not to be taken literally. *Literally* means just what it says. It's just plain talk where a word means what it says and from the context it is obvious that it is literal. For example, "The dog barked" means the dog barked. "Jesus died on the cross" means Jesus died on the cross.

While the Bible is interpreted literally, it also contains figures of speech that need to be understood from the way they are used.

There are three ways we need to investigate figurative language.

1. First we need to know if the author is using figurative language.
2. Then we need to know what kind of figurative language he is using, such as a parable, a simile, a metaphor, etc.
3. Then we need to follow the rules for the figure of speech so we can understand what the author meant by using it.

Understanding figures of speech will help us to understand the meaning of what we are studying in our Bible when we come across a passage that would not make sense if we took it literally.

Max thinks it's a great idea to get some training by looking at several different figures of speech this week. And since "M and M Detectives" are in charge of the training, we better get with it! We'll begin by looking at parables.

Molly wants to know if you recharged your batteries on your cell phone and have p __ __ __ed ? Remember, we need God's help to understand His Word. Now we're ready to begin our next adventure.

The Parable of the Shepherd

Detectives are often called on to find missing people or things. Today we are going to look at the case of the missing sheep in a parable told by Jesus.

A *parable* is a story that teaches a moral lesson or truth. Although the story is not usually a real story, it is a story that is true-to-life.

Here's the most important thing you need to remember about parables: A parable is designed to make one main point, and every detail of the parable will reinforce that main theme. So in interpreting a parable, you don't want to take each point, each detail of the parable, and try to get a specific spiritual meaning out of it. With parables, stick to the main thing, the plain thing.

Jesus used parables in His teaching for two reasons:

1. to reveal truth to believers

2. to hide truth from those who had rejected the truth and to harden their hearts against the truth (Matthew 13:10-17; Mark 4:10-12)

In order to understand the meaning of a parable, you have to:

1. Determine the occasion of the parable. By *occasion* we mean what caused Jesus to tell the story. Since parables show a specific truth, search out the WHY or WHAT of the parable. WHY was it told? WHAT brought it about?

2. Look for the meaning by examining the context of the parable. WHAT is the meaning that Jesus gives to the hearers in the parable?

3. Look for the meaning of the parable by looking at
    the customs of the people in Bible times (cultural
    context).

Okay, inductive detectives, now that we have done our
background work on parables; let's get on with the case of the
lost sheep! Turn to page 160 to our Observation Worksheet on
Luke 15. Read Luke 15:1-7 and mark the following key words:

lost (color it green)   found (finds) (color it pink)

sinner (color it brown)   rejoice (joy) (color it yellow
                                                and box it in green)

Now let's get the "occasion of this parable" by finding
out why Jesus told the parable of the lost sheep and the two
other parables that follow it. (We'll investigate the other two
parables later this week.)

First let's look at Luke 15:1.

WHO is coming to Jesus?

Tax collectors

WHY were they coming?

listen

Now read Luke 15:2.

WHAT were the Pharisees and the scribes doing?

rumbling

WHAT did they say?

_____

To WHOM did Jesus tell the parable?

_____

Now look at your Observation Worksheet where you marked your key word *lost*. WHAT was lost?

_____

Looking at your key word *rejoice*. WHO is rejoicing?

_____

WHY is he rejoicing?

_____

Were the Pharisees rejoicing? ___ Yes ___ No

WHAT were they doing? (Look at verse 2.)

_____

Luke 15:7 WHAT is there more joy in heaven over?

_____

When Jesus tells this story about the lost sheep, He is using the lost sheep as a comparison. A comparison is when you look at how things are alike. If I say, "Molly sings like a bird," then I am comparing Molly's singing to a bird's singing, which is lovely.

To WHOM are the lost sheep compared? Look at verse 7, inductive detective.

_____

And just so you don't miss our point, answer this question again:

WHAT happens in heaven when one lost sinner repents?

_____

Hey, Sam is howlin' again! A shepherd has lost his sheep, and he needs your and Sam's help. Get the shepherd through the maze to his lost sheep.

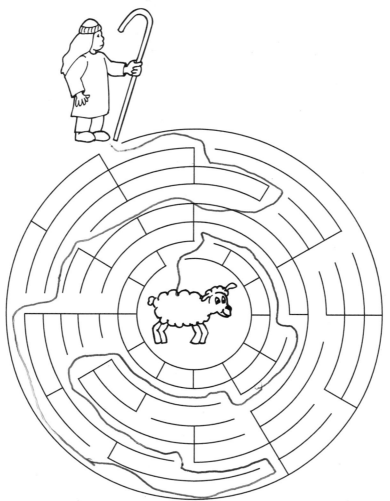

Great job! As Max and Molly said before, detectives need good memory skills to help them compile the facts for their cases. To sharpen your skills of memorization, write Luke 15:7 on an index card and read it aloud three time today (and for several more days) and you'll have it down. And God can bring it back up whenever you need it. Isn't that neat? (Did you get our figure of speech?)

"I tell you that in the same way, there will be more joy in heaven over one sinner who repents than over ninety-nine righteous persons who need no repentance"— Luke 15:7.

The Parable of the Woman

We just got word that we are needed back at the scene of Luke 15 on page 160 to do more investigating on parables.

"Molly, we need to grab our magnifying glasses and Sam's leash and head on over there. There's a woman who's lost something, and we need to find out what she's lost and how she's handling it. It will be a great exercise for our detectives-in-training. Okay, detectives, grab your cell phones. We need to put in a call to 'Central Headquarters' before we start looking at the evidence. As always, we need divine help."

Read Luke 15:8-10 and mark the same key words that we marked yesterday:

lost (color it green)	found (finds) (color it pink)
sinner (color it brown)	rejoice (joy) (color it yellow and box it in green)

Have you ever saved your money for something special and then lost part of it? How did you feel? What did you do to try and find it? Did you find it?

Let's take a look at Luke 15:8. WHAT is lost in this parable?

_____

WHAT does the woman do when she loses it?

_____

Luke 15:9 WHAT does she do when she finds it?

_____

In Luke 15:10 we see a comparison being made with the woman rejoicing in finding her lost coin.

WHO is there joy over in the presence of the angels of God?

o _____ s_____ who _____

Draw a picture of the woman with the coin that was lost. Show how she feels by giving her a happy or sad face.

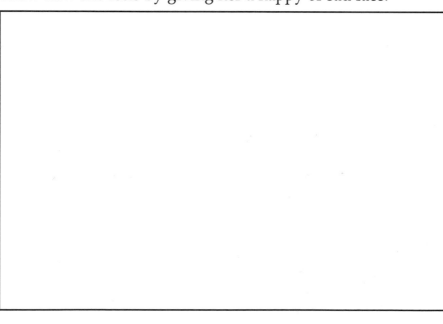

Now draw a picture of what happens in the presence of the angels of God when a sinner is saved.

How does this parable compare to the parable about the sheep? Match the things that are *alike* in each parable by connecting them with a line.

lost sheep   leaves the 99 sheep and searches for the lost sheep until found

calls friends and neighbors saying, "Rejoice with me"   lost coin

lights a lamp, sweeps house, searches carefully for coin until found   lays lamb on shoulder with rejoicing

"Hey, Molly and inductive detectives, what's up here? Maybe we're on to something!"

The Parable of the Father and His Two Sons

"Ohhhhh no, Molly, first it was lost sheep! Then a lost coin! I wonder what will be lost next?"

"I don't know, Max, but wasn't it awesome how each time there was rejoicing in finding what was lost? I'm ready to start the next case—the one about the man and his two sons. What does that story really mean, Max? Why did Jesus tell it?"

"Hmmmm, I'm not sure, Molly. But since we're investigating parables with our inductive detectives, we'll get on this one right away."

What do you think, detectives? Do you know why Jesus told this parable? I know you've heard this story a lot in Sunday school and church, but have you thought about WHY Jesus told this story? Let's find out together. We need to get on our walkie-talkies and then head back to Luke 15 on page 160. Grab those colored pencils and start your investigation by reading Luke 15:11-32 and marking the following key words again. Since we will also be marking the younger son, don't forget to mark any pronouns that refer to him.

lost (color it green)   found (finds) (color it pink)

sinner (color it brown)   rejoice (joy) (color it yellow
                                       and box it in green)

younger son (son)

Now, detectives, this case calls for some surveillance work. Keeping someone under surveillance is when a detective follows a person and watches everything he does in order to gain information about him. Let's put the younger son in this story under surveillance and see if he will help us solve our case. Get those notebooks ready so you can write down what you observe as we follow the younger brother.

Let's see, WHAT is the younger brother doing in Luke 15:12-13?

"Father, give me the _share_ of the _estate_ that falls to me."

Not many days later the younger son goes WHERE?

into a _distant_ _country_

Once he gets there, he does WHAT?

_____ his estate with

_____ _____

Oh no, detectives, it doesn't look good. This is a guy headed for trouble. First he asks for his inheritance, and then he leaves home.

Have you ever thought to yourself, "I can't wait until I'm older. Then I can do exactly what I want to do instead of what Mom and Dad tell me to do. I'll have my own money, and I'll spend it however I want to"?

I wonder if that's how the younger brother felt. After he leaves home we see him squandering (spending wastefully) all of his money. Looks like the younger brother is heading the wrong way. Stay on him and observe what happens next.

Luke 15:14-16 He becomes i_mpoverished_

and _hired_ himself to one of the citizens of

that country.

WHAT job does he take? to _feed_ the _swine_

Did anyone give him anything to eat? ___ Yes _✓_ No

Luke 15:17 Is he hungry? _✓_ Yes ___ No

WHAT do you think, detectives? It looks pretty bad, doesn't it, when you get desperate enough to want to eat what the pigs eat! Do you think the younger brother misses being at home? Keep up with him. It looks like he's had enough of the pigs, and he's heading home to his father. I wonder what his father will do when he gets there.

Luke 15:20 WHAT did the father feel when he saw his son coming home?

_He_ _felt_ _compassion_

WHAT did the father do?

_he_ _hung_ _and_ _kissed_

Luke 15:21 WHAT did the son say to his father?

"Father, I _have_ _sinned_ against

heaven and in your _sight_ ."

Luke 15:22-24 HOW did the father respond?

"For this son of mine was _dead_ and has come to

life again; he was _lost_ and has been

found . And they began to _celebrate_ ."

Luke 15:28 HOW does the older brother feel about having his brother back home?

_~~✗~~_ happy _____ sad _✓_ angry

Luke 15:31-32 WHAT reason for the celebration and rejoicing did the father give the older son?

_____

That was great surveillance work! Now let's use the evidence we gathered to see WHY Jesus told these parables.

Let's take another look at the text of Luke 15. WHAT are the key words in each parable? Tell how many times each word is used.

1. ___lost___ ___7___ times
2. ___sinners___ ___3___ times
3. ___found___ ___6___ times
4. ___rejoice___ ___3___ times

Read Luke 15:1 WHO are the people coming to hear Jesus?

___tax collectors and sinners___

Are these people Christians (saved) or sinners (lost)?

_____

Luke 15:2 Do you see any resemblance between the older brother and the Pharisees? __/__ Yes ____ No WHAT?

_____

Jesus uses the parable of the prodigal son to show the kindness of the father's heart (God's) versus the hardness of the older brother's heart (the Pharisees').

When the prodigal son came home, the father was thrilled to have his son home. He didn't care if he was filthy, smelly, and dressed in rags. He only cared that his son was found.

When we turn away from our sin and believe in Jesus, God doesn't care that we are dirty—only that we want to believe in Jesus. He loves us no matter what and wants only the best for us, just like the father wanted the best for his son. All we have to do is come home to our Father God!

We see that the older brother didn't care that his brother had returned home. His only concern was with the things his brother had done and that his dad was throwing the younger son a party. This is just like the Pharisees who were grumbling over those Jesus was eating with (the sinners and tax collectors) and what these people had done, rather than seeing the reason He was eating with them (because they were lost and needed to be saved). The Pharisees' hearts were hard like the heart of the older brother. They cared about appearances and their own selves. Jesus has the Father's heart. He cares more about the person, where the person is, and what the person needs.

Okay, detectives, how about you? Do you share Jesus with those who are different than you, like someone who dresses strange, has a weird hairdo, or looks like they need a bath? Or do you think God wouldn't want them because they don't look like you, or because they have gotten into a lot of trouble messing around with the wrong crowd? Do you think God only loves us if we haven't gotten messed up hanging around in the world's pigpen?

No

Do you have the Father's heart or the older son's? If you care more about the purple-haired kid's salvation than what he looks like, then you have the Father's heart. If you care more about what people will say if you invite this kid to church, then you have a heart like the older son's.

I have a heart like the ___Father___.

In all three of these parables you can see that Jesus is concerned with those who are lost. Once they are found, there is great rejoicing!

Why don't you pray for a kid at school or someone you know who is lost (just know that every lost person doesn't look the same). Ask God how you can share Jesus with that person. And keep on praying for him. Maybe you'll get to see him accept Jesus Christ as Savior, and then you can be the one rejoicing with God and the angels! Wouldn't that be awesome?

Keep up the good work, detectives, and don't forget to practice your memory verse!

Discover the Mystery: Symbols and Similes

"Hey, Max, look at this. Looks like we have a mystery on our hands."

"You're right, Molly. We need to get out our magnifying glasses as we search for clues to help us understand symbols and similes and how these figures of speech are used in the Bible. Why don't you tell our detectives what a symbol is, Molly?"

"A symbol is a picture or an object that stands for or represents another thing."

Okay, detectives, let's begin our search. Turn to page 163 in your Observation Worksheet on Revelation 1. Read Revelation 1:9-20 and mark the key words below to help us unlock this mystery of the lampstands and the stars:

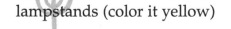

seven stars (yellow star)   lampstands (color it yellow)

mystery (color it green and put
       an orange box around it)

Now let's solve the mystery. Are these literal lampstands and stars, or are they symbols? Commissioner Context has told us. In WHAT verse did he explain the mystery?_____

Now match the symbols (the seven stars and the seven lampstands) to what they represent:

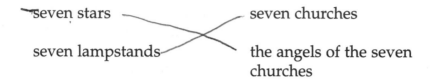

seven stars   seven churches

seven lampstands   the angels of the seven churches

"That was fun, Max! I think it's so awesome the way the Bible uses symbols to represent other things. Hey, now that our detectives know what symbols are, let's take a look at similes."

A simile is a comparison of two different things or ideas that uses connecting words. What are the connecting words? They are *like, as,* and *such as.*

Now let's look at Revelation 1 again and see if we can uncover a simile. We need to use our clue words—*like, as,* and *such as*—to help us find the similes.

There is someone in the middle of these golden lampstands. WHO is it? WHAT is He like? WHAT are the similes?

Read Revelation 1:13. Which one of our clue words is in this verse? _____

Now let's draw a picture of WHAT the one in the middle of the lampstands is like by looking at the similes.

Our first description is in Revelation 1:13: "I saw one *like* a _____ of _____."

Now draw each simile that describes the one in the middle of the lampstands in Revelation 1:13-17.

WHAT is His hair like? w_____ w_____, like s_____ Draw it on your picture.

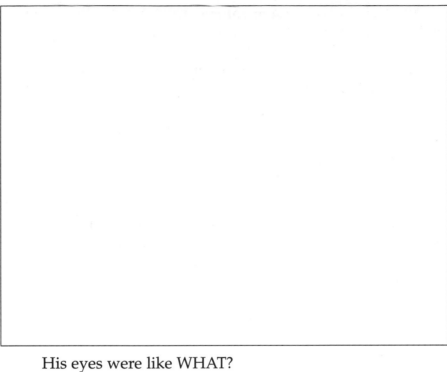

His eyes were like WHAT?

_____

WHAT were His feet like?

_____

Describe His voice.

_____

WHAT comes out of His mouth?

_____

WHAT is His face like?

_____

Now tell how John fell at His feet.

"I fell at His feet like a _____ _____."

Draw this if you want to!

Wow! What an awesome description! John must have thought so too. Why else would he fall at His feet like a dead man?

WHO is this a picture of? _____ If you are not exactly sure, read verse 18 and think about who was alive and died and is alive forever and ever and ever and ever.

Isn't that neat to have such a visual picture of how John saw J__ __ __s?

You are a doing a great job at finding clues and solving our mysteries! Before you know it, our big mystery will be solved (the mystery of how to study the Bible), and you will be a full-fledged inductive detective with Molly and Max.

Let's Figure It Out!

Molly and Max are so excited about all you've discovered this week in uncovering how the Bible uses figures of speech. We need to look at one more figure of speech before we can wrap up this investigation. Are you ready, inductive detectives? Sam is. He's scratching at the door. He loves digging for clues.

"Wait a minute, Sam. We need to make sure we're ready to begin. Pull out those walkie-talkies, detectives, and do what?

That's right! Talk to God and ask Him to guide us in our investigation.

"Now we're ready to go. Let's look at metaphors. WHAT is a metaphor? A metaphor is an implied comparison between two things that are different. If that sounds complicated, just hang on. You'll get it. Keep reading.

"A metaphor is different from a simile because it is not a stated comparison. It is a suggested or understood comparison that does *not* use the connecting words *like, as,* and *such as.* For example, 'The sky is the sea. The clouds, their ships.' What is the sky being compared to? That's right—the sea. It does not say the sky is like the sea. It suggests (or implies) it. That's a metaphor!"

Now that we know what a metaphor is, let's turn back to Revelation 1 on page 163 to find the metaphors.

Read Revelation 1:8 WHAT is the Lord God called? WHAT is the metaphor?

"I am the _____ and the _____."

Alpha is the first letter of the Greek alphabet and omega is the last letter of the Greek alphabet. The New Testament was written in Greek. In Jesus' time the people living in Israel spoke primarily Greek or Aramaic.

When God compares Himself to the alpha and omega, WHAT does this tell you about who God is? (Hint: Look at what alpha and omega mean.)

_____

Look up and read John 6:48. WHAT is Jesus being compared to?

_____

Now look up and read Ephesians 6:17. WHAT is being compared to the Word of God?

_____

Isn't it exciting the way God uses metaphors to teach us more about Him? Our investigation today has shown us that God is the beginning and the end. We see that Jesus is the bread of life—all that we need in order to live. God's Word is the sword of the Spirit, our most important weapon!

Now our case using figures of speech is solved! As we wrap up our adventure on parables, symbols, similes, and metaphors, see if you can crack the case below. Match the definition with the correct word by putting the letter of the correct definition in the blank in front of the word. Be careful! Not all the definitions will be used, and some are wrong answers. No peeking. Try to see how much you remember!

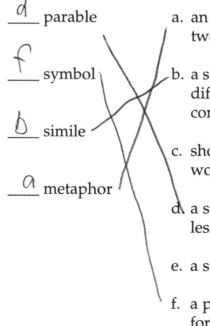

__d__ parable

__f__ symbol

__b__ simile

__a__ metaphor

a. an implied comparison between two things that are different

b. a stated comparison between two different things that uses connecting words

c. shows a contrast between two words

d. a story that teaches a moral lesson or a truth

e. a story that is a real story

f. a picture or an object that stands for or represents another thing

Now WHAT is the most helpful thing you learned from the Word of God in this week's study that you want to remember? Write it down.

_____

_____

By the way, aren't you glad that Jesus, like a shepherd, came to seek (to look for) and to save those who are lost?

4

Searching Out the Meaning

Climb back up into the tree house, inductive detectives. We need to plan how we want to handle our next case. Good detectives always have a plan. This case will help us to continue developing the skills we need in learning how to interpret the Bible. We'll need some undercover gear. There's a suspect on the loose. He claims to be a Christian, but we hear that his deeds aren't like those of a real believer in Jesus Christ. He seems to be sinning all the time just like he did before he said he became a Christian. And he is so hateful to other Christians. So grab those sunglasses and put a call into "Central Headquarters." Then we're ready to start our next assignment: interpretation.

What do our observations tell us? What do they mean? Can a person's deeds, the way he lives, really show us if he is a true believer or a false believer? We're going to dig into this case a little deeper by learning how to search out the meaning of something through Greek words, verb tenses, and cross-references.

On the Trail

Now that we've talked to "Central Headquarters," we need to get out our notebooks. Before we begin to tail our suspect, we need to get the facts. Let's lay our groundwork first by turning to page 167 to our Observation Worksheet on 1 John 3. Now read 1 John 3:1-10 and mark every reference to the *children of God* by coloring it orange. When you finish, put down the number of verses where the words *children of God* are found: _____

Great! You found the children of God, but WHO else's children were mentioned in verse 10? _____

Boy, look at what you just uncovered, inductive detective: children of God *and* children of the devil!
When you remember what you learned about observation, what is this (the children of God *and* the children of the devil)?
Circle the correct word. It is a:

simile   comparison   contrast   metaphor   parable

Now let's see if the text tells us anything more about the children of God and the children of the devil. We'd better make some careful observations before we do any interpretation.
First read through the verses again and mark every reference to the *devil* with a red pitchfork like this:

Next mark *born of God* in verse 9 by coloring it yellow. When you finish, record what you learn below:

"No one who is born of God _____ _____."

That is quite a statement, isn't it? Before we decide what it means we will have to do some further investigation. But before we do, let's see if these verses mention *sin* anywhere else. Read 1 John 3:1-10 and color every reference to *sin* brown.

Wow! *Sin* sure is used a lot of times, isn't it? And you just saw that someone who is really born of God, and is God's child doesn't practice sin. Maybe the clues we've uncovered about *sin* will help us to see who is a true believer and who is a false believer. Let's use the clues to make a list and compare the true believer to the false believer.

A True Believer (Child of God)

verse 6   a_____ in Him and does not s_____

verse 7   practices r_____, is

              r_____

verse 9   _____ of G_____ because His

           s_____ a_____ in him and he cannot s_____

False Believer (Child of the Devil)

verse 4   practices _____ and practices l_____

verse 6   has not s _____ Him or k_____ Him

verse 8   of the d_____

verse 10 does not practice r_____, does not

              l_____ his b_____

"Watch out, Max, you stepped on a clue!"

"Aha! Another secret message. Let's decode it to see if it can help us in our investigation to find out how to know a true child of God from a child of the devil."

Use the following key to help you decode the secret message.

A ❤	B ■	C ✪	D ▲
E ✳	F ⟟	G ▼	H 🏃
I ☾	J $	K †	L ☕
M ✉	N ☆	O ☁	P 📌
Q ✿	R 👤	S 🐦	T 🐄
U ❀	V ✎	W ✻	X ✧
Y ✿	Z ◎		

Here's the message:

■ ✿   🐄 🏃 ☾ 🐦   🐄 🏃 ✳   ✪ 🏃 ☾ ☕ ▲ 👤 ✳ ☆

_b_ _y_   T H I S   T H E   C H I _ _ _ _ _

☁ ⟟   ▼ ☁ ▲   ❤ ☆ ▲   🐄 🏃 ✳

_ _   _ _ _   _ _ _

✪ 🏃 ☾ ☕ ▲ 👤 ✳ ☆   ☁ ⟟   🐄 🏃 ✳   ▲ ✳ ✎ ☾ ☕

_ _ _ _ _ _ _ _   _ _   _ _ _   _ _ _ _ _

❤ 👤 ✳   ☁ ■ ☾ ☁ ❀ 🐦   ❤ ☆ ✿ ☁ ☆ ✳

_ _ _   _ _ _ _ _ _ :   _ _ _ _ _ _

✳ 🏃 ☁   ▲ ☁ ✳ 🐦   ☆ ☁ 🐄   📌 👤 ❤ ✪ 🐄 ☾ ✪ ✳

_ _ _   _ _ _ _ _   _ _ _   _ _ _ _ _ _ _

👤 ☾ ▼ 🏃 🐄 ✳ ☁ ❀ 🐦 ☆ ✳ 🐄   ☾ 🐦   ☆ ☁ 🐄

_ _ _ _ _ _ _ _ _ _ _ _ _   _ _   _ _ _

☁ ⟟   ▼ ☁ ▲   ☆ ☁ 👤   🐄 🏃 ✳   ☁ ☆ ✳

_ _   _ _ _ ,   _ _ _   _ _ _   _ _ _

✳ 🧍 ☁　　▲ ☁ ✳ 🦆　　⭐ ☁ 🌴　　🍵 ☁ 〰️✳　　🧍 ☾ 🦆

___ ___ ___　　___ ___ ___ ___　　___ ___ ___　　___ ___ ___ ___　　___ ___ ___

■ 👤 ☁ 🦆 🧍 ✳ 👤

___ ___ ___ ___ ___ ___ ___

1 John 3:____

Have you read that before? Where? Write it down: 1 John 3:____. Now write this message (your memory verse) on an index card and practice saying it three times aloud. Way to go! Tomorrow we'll investigate this case further.

In Pursuit

Today we will pursue this issue of sin because 1 John 3:10 tells us that no one who is born of God, who is a child of God, practices sin! So, inductive detectives, we need to find out what John means when he talks about sin in 1 John 3. We need to have the correct interpretation. To find out the meaning of *sin,* Bible detectives can do a word study. A word study is the study of words in the original languages of the Old and New Testaments.

First let's look at how the Bible was written. The Bible tells us in 2 Timothy 3:16 (our first memory verse) that "All Scripture is _____ by God." The Holy Spirit moved and guided men to write what God wanted them to say. The Bible doesn't contain God's words; *it is* the Word of God.

In early history the writing was done on stone, clay tablets, leather (animal skins), and papyrus scrolls. Eventually, the scrolls were replaced by the *codex*. The codex was made from folded sheets, called *quires*, which were stitched together like a book.

The copies of the Old Testament were transcribed (written) by hand. The men who did the transcribing were called *scribes*. If just one error was found, then the whole copy was destroyed.
Isn't that amazing!

Did you know that the Old Testament was written primarily in Hebrew with some Aramaic, and then it was translated into Koine Greek? The New Testament was written in Koine Greek because Koine Greek was the common language that was used in the lands where the books of the New Testament were written during the time of the Roman Empire.

Now that we know how the Bible was written, let's look at why we want to do a word study. When we do a word study, we look at the word in the original language in which it was written to help us to understand what the authors meant when they used that word. It also helps us get the full meaning of the word, which can be very helpful when we come across a passage that is not easily understood. It also helps us see how that word is used in other Scriptures.

Two helpful tools for doing word studies are an exhaustive concordance and an expository dictionary. There is also a computer program available that has an exhaustive concordance on it. It's one that a lot of grown-ups use to help them do word studies and mark their key words. It is called *Bible Companion Series, The Inductive Study Edition.*

An exhaustive concordance is a book that shows us where each word in a certain translation (like the King James Version, the New American Standard Bible, or the New International Version) is used throughout the Bible. It shows all the references to *all* the words in a given translation. There are several exhaustive concordances that you can use: *Strong's Exhaustive Concordance,* the *New American Standard Exhaustive Concordance,* and the *NIV Exhaustive Concordance.* Looking up a word in a concordance will help you to discover the original meaning or use of a word.

This is a really involved mystery that not many adults know how to solve. So be patient, inductive detectives, and don't give up.

"Molly, do you have our sunglasses? It's time for our undercover work."

"Where's Sam?"

"Come on, Sam, ol' boy. We know that's you behind those shades! We need you. It's time to hit the streets. We need to track down our suspect *sin.* We also need to see if *sin* has an 'alias' that he goes by!"

As Max mentioned the word *alias,* Sam cocked his head. "*Alias,* Sam, ol' boy, means WHAT other name does *sin* go by? The last report we have on *sin* is that he was seen heading down Standard Avenue—under an assumed name, of course!"

WHAT is *sin's* real name? Let's find out. The pages we'll use are taken out of the *New American Standard Exhaustive Concordance.* The *Concordance* is divided into two sections: the concordance, which is located in the front of the book, and the Hebrew and Greek dictionaries, which are located in the back. The concordance has the Scripture reference for every word in the Bible. The dictionaries have the Hebrew (Old Testament) and Greek (New Testament) words and their definitions. If your mom or dad has a *New American Standard Exhaustive Concordance,* you may want to do your training in it. Otherwise, everything you need to track down *sin's* alias is on page 81.

How to use the concordance:

Step 1: Look up the English word *(sin)* in the concordance (or page 81 of this book). Find the Scripture reference (1 John 3:4) where that word *(sin)* is used. Then find the number code.

Step 2: Turn to the back of the concordance (or to page 82 in this book) to the Greek dictionary because we are looking for a word in the New Testament. We would use the Hebrew dictionary if we were looking for a word in the Old Testament.

Step 3: Find the number code and the Greek word (or Hebrew word).

The definition for that word will be in italic type, before the colon and dash (:—).

Okay, detectives, you've arrived on Standard Avenue. Why don't you conduct a house-to-house search to find *sin*'s real name. The first house is located on the next page.

WHAT Scripture reference are we using? 1 John 3:4

WHAT is *sin*'s number code? _____

WHAT is *sin*'s other number code that is used in 1 John 2:1? _____

New American Standard Exhaustive Concordance

Sin

I have not allowed my mouth to **s**	Jb 31:30	2398	the world, and death through **s**,	Ro 5:12	266
'For he adds rebellion to his **s**;	Jb 34:37	2403b	until the Law **s** was in the world,	Ro 5:13	266
Tremble, and do not **s**;	Ps 4:4	2398	but **s** is not imputed when there is	Ro 5:13	266
is forgiven, Whose **s** is covered!	Ps 32:1	2401	but where **s** increased, grace	Ro 5:20	266
When I kept silent *about my* **s**,	Ps 32:3		that, as **s** reigned in death, even	Ro 5:21	266
I acknowledged my **s** to You,	Ps 32:5	2403b	Are we to continue in **s** so that grace	Ro 6:1	266
forgave the guilt of my **s**.	Ps 32:5	2403b	How shall we who died to **s** still live	Ro 6:2	266
in my bones because of my **s**.	Ps 38:3	2403b	body of **s** might be done away with,	Ro 6:6	266
full of anxiety because of my **s**.	Ps 38:18	2403b	we would no longer be slaves to **s**;	Ro 6:6	266
That I may not **s** with my tongue;	Ps 39:1	2398	he who has died is freed from **s**.	Ro 6:7	266
Burnt offering and **s** offering You	Ps 40:6	2401	death that He died, He died to **s** once	Ro 6:10	266
And cleanse me from my **s**.	Ps 51:2	2403b	consider yourselves to be dead to **s**,	Ro 6:11	266
And my **s** is ever before me.	Ps 51:3	2403b	Therefore do not let **s** reign in	Ro 6:12	266
And in **s** my mother conceived me.	Ps 51:5	2399	the members of your body to **s** *as*	Ro 6:13	266
for my transgression nor for my **s**,	Ps 59:3	2403b	**s** shall not be master over you,	Ro 6:14	266
On account of the **s** of their mouth	Ps 59:12	2403b	Shall we **s** because we are not	Ro 6:15	264
still continued to **s** against Him,	Ps 78:17	2398	either of **s** resulting in death,	Ro 6:16	266
You covered all their **s**.	Ps 85:2	2403b	that though you were slaves of **s**,	Ro 6:17	266
And let his prayer become **s**.	Ps 109:7	2401	and having been freed from **s**,	Ro 6:18	266
s of his mother be blotted out.	Ps 109:14	2403b	For when you were slaves of **s**,	Ro 6:20	266
That I may not **s** against You.	Ps 119:11	2398	freed from **s** and enslaved to God,	Ro 6:22	266
be held with the cords of his **s**.	Pr 5:22	2403b	For the wages of **s** is death,	Ro 6:23	266
Fools mock at **s**, But among the	Pr 14:9	817	Is the Law **s**? May it never be!	Ro 7:7	266
But **s** is a disgrace to *any* people.	Pr 14:34	2403b	I would not have come to know **s**	Ro 7:7	266
my heart, I am pure from my **s**"?	Pr 20:9	2403b	But **s**, taking opportunity through	Ro 7:8	266
The lamp of the wicked, is **s**.	Pr 21:4	2403b	for apart from the Law **s** *is* dead.	Ro 7:8	266
The devising of folly is **s**,	Pr 24:9	2403b	commandment came, **s** became alive	Ro 7:9	266
Do not let your speech cause you to **s**	Ec 5:6	2398	for **s**, taking an opportunity through	Ro 7:11	266
they display their **s** like Sodom;	Is 3:9	2403b	Rather it was **s**, in order that it	Ro 7:13	266
And **s** as if with cart ropes,"	Is 5:18	2403a	shown to be **s** by effecting my death	Ro 7:13	266
away and your **s** is forgiven."	Is 6:7	2403b	**s** would become utterly sinful.	Ro 7:13	266
price of the pardoning of his **s**:	Is 27:9	2403b	of flesh, sold into bondage to **s**.	Ro 7:14	266
Spirit, In order to add **s** to sin;	Is 30:1	2403b	doing it, but **s** which dwells in me.	Ro 7:17	266
Spirit, In order to add sin to **s**;	Is 30:1	2403b	it, but **s** which dwells in me.	Ro 7:20	266
sinful hands have made for you as a **s**.	Is 31:7	2399	law of **s** which is in my members.	Ro 7:23	266
Yet He Himself bore the **s** of many,	Is 53:12	2399	other, with my flesh the law of **s**.	Ro 7:25	266
or what is our **s** which we have	Jer 16:10	2403b	from the law of **s** and of death.	Ro 8:2	266
repay their iniquity and their **s**,	Jer 16:18	2403b	flesh and *as an offering* for	Ro 8:3	266
The **s** of Judah is written down	Jer 17:1	2403b	sin, He condemned **s** in the flesh,	Ro 8:3	266
for **s** throughout your borders.	Jer 17:3	2403b	the body is dead because of **s**,	Ro 8:10	266
blot out their **s** from Your sight.	Jer 18:23	2403b	whatever is not from faith is **s**.	Ro 14:23	266
their **s** I will remember no more."	Jer 31:34	2403b	Every *other* **s** that a man commits	1Co 6:18	265
to c⌒ to ⌒	Jer ⌒	2398	do what he wishes, he does not **s**;	1Co 7:36	264
			it is weak, you **s** against Christ.	1Co 8:12	264
			The sting of death is **s**,	1Co 15:56	266
⌒ my so⌒			power of **s** i⌒ e law;	1Co 15:56	266
⌒salem, for **s** and for impurity.	⌒	⌒b	Him ⌒ w no **s** *to be*	2Co 5:21	266
any **s** and blasphemy shall be	Mt 12:31	266	⌒ur b⌒		266
"Lord, how often shall my brother **s**	Mt 18:21	264	whic⌒ ⌒ay c⌒		
but is guilty of an eternal **s**"	Mk 3:29	265	blood i⌒ our striving again⌒	H⌒	
who takes away the **s** of the world!	Jn 1:29	266	high priest *as an offering* for **s**,		
do not **s** anymore, so that nothing	Jn 5:14	264	conceived, it gives birth to **s**;	Jas 1:15	
"He who is without **s** among you,	Jn 8:7	361	and when **s** is accomplished, it	Jas 1:15	266
From now on **s** no more."]	Jn 8:11	264	you are committing **s** *and are*	Jas 2:9	266
seek Me, and will die in your **s**;	Jn 8:21	266	does not do it, to him it is **s**.	Jas 4:17	266
everyone who commits **s** is the slave	Jn 8:34	266	you **s** and are harshly treated,	1Pe 2:20	264
who commits sin is the slave of **s**.	Jn 8:34	266	WHO COMMITTED NO **S**,	1Pe 2:22	266
"Which one of you convicts Me of **s**?	Jn 8:46	266	that we might die to **s** and live to	1Pe 2:24	266
were blind, you would have no **s**;	Jn 9:41	266	in the flesh has ceased from **s**,	1Pe 4:1	266
'We see,' your **s** remains.	Jn 9:41	266	adultery that never cease from **s**,	2Pe 2:14	266
to them, they would not have **s**,	Jn 15:22	266	His Son cleanses us from all **s**.	1Jn 1:7	266
they have no excuse for their **s**.	Jn 15:22	266	If we say that we have no **s**,	1Jn 1:8	266
else did, they would not have **s**;	Jn 15:24	266	things to you so that you may not **s**.	1Jn 2:1	264
convict the world concerning **s** and	Jn 16:8	266	Everyone who practices **s** also	1Jn 3:4	266
concerning **s**, because they do not	Jn 16:9	266	and **s** is lawlessness.	1Jn 3:4	266
Me to you has *the* greater **s**."	Jn 19:11	266	and in Him there is no **s**.	1Jn 3:5	266
do not hold this **s** against them!"	Ac 7:60	266	one who practices **s** is of the devil,	1Jn 3:8	266
Jews and Greeks are all under **s**;	Ro 3:9	266	one who is born of God practices **s**,	1Jn 3:9	266
the Law *comes* the knowledge of **s**.	Ro 3:20	266	and he cannot **s**, because he is	1Jn 3:9	264
"BLESSED IS THE MAN WHOSE **S** THE	Ro 4:8	266	sees his brother committing a **s**	1Jn 5:16	266
one man **s** entered into the world,	Ro 5:12	266	who commit **s** *not leading* to death.	1Jn 5:16	264
			There is a **s** *leading* to death;	1Jn 5:16	266
			All unrighteousness is **s**,	1Jn 5:17	266
			there is a **s** not *leading* to death.	1Jn 5:17	266

Now head to the back room to look at *sin's* files.
Use the Greek dictionary below to look for *sin's* number 266.

237b - 316 ἀλλαχοῦ - ἀναγκαῖος	**GREEK DICTIC**

237b. ἀλλαχοῦ allachou; from *243*; else-where:— somewhere else(1).

238. ἀλληγορέω allēgoreō; from *243* and ἀγορεύω agoreuō (*to speak in an assembly*); to speak allegorically:— allegorically speaking(1).

239. ἀλληλουϊά hallēlouia; of Heb. or., im-per. of [*1984b, 3050*]; hallelujah, alleluia (an adoring exclamation):— hallelujah(4).

240. ἀλλήλων allēlōn; gen. pl. of a recip. pron. having no nom.; *of one another:*— each (1), each of us by the other's(1), each other(1), one another(90), one another's(2), themselves (1), together*(2), yourselves(1).

241. ἀλλογενής allogenēs; from *243* and *1085*; *of another race:*— foreigner(1).

242. ἅλλομαι hallomai; from a prim. root ἁλ hal; *to leap:*— leaped(1), leaping(1), springing (1).

243. ἄλλος allos; a prim. word; *other, anoth-er:*— another(52), another's(1), another man(2), another woman(2), else(4), more(5), one(2), one another(1), one else(1), other(37), other man(1), other men(1), other women(1), others(41), some (4), someone else(m)(3).

264. ἁμαρτάνω hamartanō; from a prim. root αμαρτ amart; *to miss the mark, err, sin:*— commit sin(1), committed offense(1), commit-ting(m)(1), sin(11), sinned(17), sinning(4), sins (8).

265. ἁμάρτημα hamartēma; from *264*; a *sin:*— sin(2), sins(2).

266. ἁμαρτία hamartia; from *264*; a *missing the mark:*— sin(96), sinful(3), sins(75).

267. ἁμάρτυρος amarturos; from *1* (as a neg. pref.) and *3144*; *without witness:*— without wit-ness(1).

268. ἁμαρτωλός hamartōlos; from *264*; *sin-ful:*— sinful(3), sinner(12), sinners(31).

269. ἄμαχος amachos; from *1* (as a neg. pref.) and *3163*; *abstaining from fighting:*— unconten-tious(2).

270. ἀμάω amaō; from a prim. root μα ma; *to reap:*— mowed(1).

271. ἀμέθυστος amethustos; from *1* (as a neg. pref.) and *3184*; *amethyst:*— amethyst(1).

272. ἀμελέω ameleō; from *1* (as a neg. pref.) and *3199*; *to be careless:*— care(1), neglect(2), paid no attention(1).

WHAT can you tell us about number 266? WHAT is *sin's* real name? ha __ __ __ __ __ a

WHAT is *hamartia*? It means "a missing the mark." It is a noun. A noun names a person, place, or thing.

Now check out number 264. WHAT is 264's name? ha __ __ __ __ __ __ o

WHAT is *hamartano*? It means "to miss the mark." It is a verb. A verb usually shows action.

When we sin we miss the mark, just like the arrow misses the bull's-eye below.

Great work! You are hot on *sin*'s trail. We'll pick up our investigation tomorrow. Don't forget to practice your memory verse!

The Investigation of Verbs

Okay, inductive detectives, gather around. We need to brainstorm before we hit the streets again. Yesterday we saw that number 264 is a verb that means to miss the mark. Today we are going to investigate the tenses of Greek verbs. The tenses of Greek verbs show the kind of action of the verb. We are only going to investigate three major verb tenses that will show us if it is a continuing action, an action, or an action in the past with the results continuing in the present. Printed out on the next page is 1 John 3:4-10. Molly has put each verb in italics, and underneath each verb she has written what tense it is, using the three tenses that we will investigate.

4 Everyone who *practices* sin also *practices* lawlessness;
       (present)   (present)

and sin *is* lawlessness. 5 You know that He *appeared* in
       (present)   (aorist)

order to *take away* sins; and in Him there *is* no sin.
        (aorist)   (present)

6 No one who *abides* in Him *sins*; no one who *sins has seen*
             (present)   (present)   (present) (perfect)

Him or *knows* Him. 7 Little children, make sure no one
       (present)

deceives you; the one who *practices* righteousness *is*
(present)   (present)   (present)

righteous, just as He *is* righteous; 8 the one who *practices*
                      (present)   (present)

sin *is* of the devil; for the devil *has sinned* from the
    (present)   (present)

beginning. The Son of God *appeared* for this purpose, to
                          (aorist)

destroy the works of the devil. 9 No one who *is born* of
(aorist)   (perfect)

God *practices* sin, because His seed *abides* in him; and he
    (present)   (present)

cannot *sin*, because he *is born* of God. 10 By this the
       (present)   (perfect)

children of God and the children of the devil *are* obvious:
                                              (present)

anyone who *does not practice* righteousness *is* not of God,
           (present)   (present)

nor the one who *does not love* his brother.
                (present)

Have you ever seen Morse code? It is a way of sending a message by using dots • and long lines (dashes) — to represent letters. Let's make up a code using dots • and long lines — to show different verb tenses. Then we can signal each other as to whether something simply happened, whether it is going on continuously (habitually), or whether it happened in the past and continues to be true!

Our first verb tense is the **present tense.** Present tense tells that this is an action that is continuous. It keeps on happening. Such as:

Molly *is practicing* ballet.

Show the present tense in our code like this: — (one long line) to help you remember it is a continuous action. Let's develop a detective signal for these verbs so we could just signal our partner with our foot as to when something happened. This will be a cool way for us to communicate with each other. If you want to tell each other something has been going on and on, just subtly slide your foot across the floor in a straight line.

An example of a verb in the present tense is found in 1 John 3:8: "The one who *practices* sin is of the devil; for the devil has sinned from the beginning. The Son of God appeared for this purpose, to destroy the works of the devil." This verb *practices* is in the present tense. *Practices sin* is a continuing action as a habit of their life.

Our next verb tense is **aorist tense.** It is an action that happened. When it happened is not the issue.

Molly *practiced* ballet.

Show the aorist tense in our code like this: • (a dot) to help you remember that it happened. To do the action, just tap your foot once on the floor. Your observant partner will get the point!

An example of a verb in the aorist tense is also found in 1 John 3:8. The verb *destroy* is in the aorist tense. It happened at one point in time.

The last tense that we are going to investigate is the **perfect tense.** Perfect tense tells us the action has happened in the past with results that are continuing to the present. Such as:

Molly is good at ballet, *having practiced* for years.

Show the perfect tense in our code like this: • — (a dot and a long line) to help you remember that it happened at one point in time and is continuing to happen. To do the action, tap your foot once on the floor and then slide it in a straight line (like you do for present tense). Look kinda cool when you do. Remember, it's an inductive detective signal!

An example of this tense is found in 1 John 3:9: "No one who *is born* of God practices sin, because His seed abides in him; and he cannot sin, because he is *born* of God."

Being *born* of God happens at one point in our life. When we are saved we are born of God. But it also has a continuing result. Isn't that wonderful?

Now that we have learned these tenses, let's see how knowing them would help with interpretation. By looking at the tenses in 1 John 3:6,8,9,10 we see that real Christians cannot sin continuously as a habit of life because God's seed, Jesus, abides continuously in true Christians. But can Christians sin? Look at 1 John 2:1-2 printed out below.

> *"My little children, I am* writing *[**present tense**] these things to you so that you* may not *[**aorist tense**] sin. And if anyone* sins *[**aorist tense**], we* have *[**present tense**] an Advocate with the Father, Jesus Christ the righteous; and He Himself* is *[**present tense**] the propitiation for our sins; and not for ours only, but also for those of the whole world."*

Now let's interrogate (question) the text above (1 John 2:1-2) to find out the meaning.

1. To WHOM is John writing?

his children

Color every reference to the recipients orange (including *our*) and color every reference to *sin* brown. Then list what you see about the recipients.

Recipients

verse 1 called my "*little* *children*"

writing you so that you *may* *not* *sin*

verse 2 "If anyone sins we have an *advokit* with the Father."

J*esus* C*hrist* is the p*ropaciate* for our sins.

2. According to this, can a Christian sin? ✓ Yes ___ No

3. But what is the tense? *aorist tense*

Therefore, from this passage we see that a Christian can commit single acts of sin, but he or she cannot sin habitually. This is where we see the importance of context and interpreting God's Word correctly.

Does 1 John answer this question about if a Christian can sin habitually? Of course! See if you can find the answer by going back and reading 1 John 3:4-10 and checking out the verb tenses on page 84.

WHAT verse gives you the answer as to whether or not a real believer, a child of God, can sin habitually (practice sin)? _____

Now, on your own, write out the part of the verse that proves your point.

_____

_____

Now that you have seen how important verb tenses are, let's test what you've learned.

WHAT tense keeps on happening?

_____*present*_____

Write the code and do the action.

WHAT tense happens in the past?

_____*aorist*_____

Write the code and do the action.

WHAT tense happens in the past but has a continuous result?

_____*perfect*_____

Write the code and do the action.

What an investigation! You're going to make a great inductive detective!

Back on the Trail

It's good to have you back at the tree house. Let's make a call to "Central Headquarters" to ask for help in continuing our investigation on *sin*. Today we'll gather more information on our suspect *sin* by using another tool: an expository dictionary. We'll use Zodhiates' *The Complete Word Study Dictionary* and *Vine's Expository Dictionary*. An expository dictionary gives a more detailed definition than those that are found in dictionaries in the back of the concordance. To use Zodhiates' dictionary, you will need to know your number code on *sin* that you found by using your concordance.

Now are you ready to continue in the pursuit of your suspect *sin*? Molly just received word that after *sin* left Standard Avenue he made a right turn at the light.

Remember as you continue your search that *sin's* real name is *hamartia*. Wait! Sam is sounding the alarm. Look up ahead. I think *sin* just ducked into Zodhiates' Bookstore. Why don't we head into Zodhiates' Bookstore and see what else we can learn about *sin*?

Look at the pages that follow and then go to page 93 to find out what to do.

Zodhiates' Dictionary

129   ἁμάρτημα (265)

and should not be translated "fadeth not." The word is *amarántinos* and does not refer to the quality of the heavenly inheritance as not fading away, but rather to the makeup of the crown itself as being of amaranths, unfading flowers.

Syn.: *amárantos* (263), unfading; *áphthartos* (862), incorruptible; *amíantos* (283), unsoiled, undefiled.

263. ἀμάραντος amárantos; gen. *amarántou*, masc.–fem., neut. *amáranton*, adj. from the priv. *a* (1), without, and *maraínō* (3133), to fade. Unfading, only in 1 Pet. 1:4. Our heavenly inheritance is not something beautiful which lasts only for a while and then fades away. It is of unfailing loveliness, reserved for the faithful in heaven. The fabled flower that did not fade away was an amaranth (*amárantos*) in contrast to the ordinary grass (*chórtos* [5528]) which fades, falls away, and dies quickly (Job 14:2; Ps. 37:2; 103:15; Is. 40:6, 7; Matt. 6:30; James 1:11; 1 Pet. 1:24). Another Gr. word, *amarántinos* (262), is unfortunately translated "that fadeth not away" (1 Pet. 5:4) which corresponds more to the meaning of *amárantos*, spoken of the quality of the crown of glory. The suffix –*inos* in *amarántinos* indicates the substance of which something is made and not the quality of it as does *amárantos*. The crown of glory will be *amarántinos*, made up of amaranths or the fabled, unfading flowers. The heavenly inheritance of the believer does not decay for it is *amárantos*. Corruption cannot touch it or ever wear out its freshness, brightness, and beauty. See also *amíantos* (283), undefiled.

264. ἀμαρτάνω hamartánō; fut. *hamartḗsō*, aor. *hēmártēsa*; 2d aor. *hḗmarton*. To sin, to miss a mark on the way, not to hit the mark. One who keeps missing the mark in his relationship to God is *hamartōlós* (268), sinner.

(I) To err, swerve from the truth, go wrong, used in an absolute sense in 1 Cor. 15:34, meaning to beware lest one be drawn into errors pertaining to faith, of which the Apostle is speaking (Titus 3:11).

(II) To err in action, in respect to a prescribed law, i.e., to commit errors, to do wrong, sin.

(A) Generally, to sin, spoken of any sin, used in an absolute sense (Matt. 27:4; John 5:14; 8:11; 9:2, 3; Rom. 2:12; 3:23; 5:12, 14, 16; 6:15; 1 Cor. 7:28, 36; Eph. 4:26; 1 Tim. 5:20; Heb. 3:17; 10:26; 1 Pet. 2:20; 2 Pet. 2:4; 1 John 1:10; 2:1; 3:6, 8, 9; 5:16, 18. In 1 John 5:16, to sin a sin. Sept.: Ex. 32:30; Lev. 4:14, 23, 28).

(B) With *eis* (1519), unto, with the acc. to sin against anyone, to offend, wrong (Matt. 18:15, 21; Luke 15:18, 21; 17:3, 4; Acts 25:8; 1 Cor. 6:18; 8:12; Sept.: Gen. 20:6, 9; 43:9; 1 Sam. 2:25).

(C) To "sin before someone" means to do evil in the sight of anyone, to sin against, to wrong (Luke 15:21; Sept.: Gen. 39:9; Deut. 1:41; 20:18; 1 Sam. 7:6; 12:23; 14:33, 34). See *hamartía* (266), sin, which has many syn. listed; *hamártēma* (265), an individual deed or sin; *anamártētos* (361), without sin; *proamartánō* (4258), to sin previously.

Deriv.: *amártēma* (265), sin; *hamartía* (266), sin, sinful; *hamartōlós* (268), a sinner; *anamártētos* (361), without sin; *proamartánō* (4258), to sin previously.

Syn.: *ptaíō* (4417), to stumble, offend; *adikéō* (91), to do wrong; *skandalízō* (4624), to offend, be a stumblingblock to someone, trip someone; *astochéō* (795), to miss the goal; *parabaínō* (3845), to transgress; *píptō* (4098), to fall; *parapíptō* (3895), to fall away; *paranoméō* (3891), to go contrary to law; *peripíptō* (4045), to fall by the side; *planáomai* (4105), to go astray.

Ant.: *orthopodéō* (3716), to walk uprightly; *akolouthéō* (190), to follow.

265. ἁμάρτημα hamártēma; gen. *hamartḗmatos*, neut. noun from *hamartánō* (264), to sin. Deed of disobedience to a divine law, a mistake, miss, error, transgression, sin (Mark 3:28; 4:12; Rom. 3:25; 1 Cor. 6:18; Sept.: Gen. 31:36; Is. 58:1).

άμαρτία (266)   **130**

Nouns ending in *–ma* indicate the result of a certain action, in this case *hamartía* (266), sin. *Hamártēma* is sin as an individual act.

Syn.: *paráptōma* (3900), the deed of trespassing, a trespass; *adíkēma* (92), a wrong, an iniquity perpetrated; *agnóēma* (51), shortcoming, error, a thing ignored; *opheílēma* (3783), that which one owes, a debt; *hếttēma* (2275), a loss, defeat, defect; *plánē* (4106), deceit, delusion.

Ant.: *akríbeia* (195), exactness; *asphá- leia* (803), safety; *alếtheia* (225), truth; *epanórthōsis* (1882), rectification, cor- rection.

266. άμαρτία *hamartía*; gen. *hamartías*, fem. noun from *hamartánō* (264), to sin. Sin, missing the true end and scope of our lives, which is God. An offense in relation to God with emphasis on guilt.

(I) Aberration from the truth, error (John 8:46 where it stands as the opposite of *alếtheia* [225], truth. See also John 16:8, 9).

(II) Aberration from a prescribed law or rule of duty, whether in general or of particular sins.

(A) Generally (Matt. 3:6; 9:2, 5, 6; Mark 1:4, 5; 1 Cor. 15:3; Heb. 4:15; Sept.: Gen. 15:16; 18:20; Is. 53:5). "Thou art wholly born in sin" (a.t.; John 9:34) means thou art a sinner from the womb (cf. Ps. 51:5; 58:3; Is. 48:8). To "commit sin" (a.t.; 2 Cor. 11:7; 1 Pet. 2:22; 1 John 3:9) means the same thing as to work sin (James 2:9). In 1 John 5:16, to "sin a sin" means to commit any sin. In the gen. after another noun, *hamartía* often supplies the place of an adj. meaning sinful, wicked, impious. In 2 Thess. 2:3, the "man of sin" means the Antichrist. In Rom. 7:5, "the passions of sins" (a.t.) means sinful de- sires. In Heb. 10:6, 8 and 13:11, "con- cerning sin" (a.t.) refers to sacrifice for sin. In Heb. 10:26, "offering for sin" (a.t.) refers to those who sin willfully (see also Heb. 10:18; Sept.: Lev. 5:8; Ps. 40:7).

(B) Spoken of particular sins, e.g., of unbelief (John 8:21, 24); of lewdness (2 Pet. 2:14); of defection from the gospel of Christ (Heb. 11:25; 12:1).

(C) By metonymy, of abstraction for concrete, *hamartía* for *hamartōlós* (268), sinner meaning sinful, i.e., either as caus- ing sin (Rom. 7:7, "Is the law the cause of sin?" [a.t.]) or as committing sin (2 Cor. 5:21 meaning He has been treated as if He were a sinner). In Heb. 12:4, it refers to the adversaries of the gospel.

(D) By metonymy, the practice of sin- ning, habit of sin (Rom. 3:9; 5:12, 20, 21; Gal. 3:22).

(E) By metonymy, proneness to sin, sinful desire or propensity (John 8:34; Rom. 6:1, 2, 6, 12, 14; 7:7ff.; Heb. 3:13, "the deceitfulness of our sinful propensi- ties" [a.t.]).

(III) The imputation or consequences of sin, the guilt and punishment of sin as in the phrase "to take away [or bear] sin" (a.t.), i.e., the imputation of it (John 1:29; Rom. 11:27; Heb. 9:26; 10:11; 1 Pet. 2:24; 1 John 3:5). To remit (*aphíēmi* [863]) sins and the remission (*áphesis* [859]) of sins means to remove the guilt, punishment, and power of sin (Matt. 9:2, 5, 6; 26:28; Luke 7:47–49; John 20:23; Heb. 10:4). In John 9:41, "your sin remains" (a.t.) means your guilt and exposure to punishment remain (cf. John 15:22, 24; 1 John 1:9). In 1 Cor. 15:17, "ye are yet in your sins" means you are still under the guilt and power of your sins. In Heb. 9:28, "with- out sin" means He shall appear the second time but not for the putting away of the consequences of sin (Heb. 9:26; Sept.: Lev. 22:9; Num. 9:13; Prov. 10:16; Is. 5:18; 53:6, 11; Lam. 3:39; Ezek. 3:20; Zech. 14:19). See *hamártēma* (265), sin as an individual act, a determination of the nature of man as a personal power and also used of individual acts. Used in an ab- solute or relative sense. Individual sins do not annul the general character or the actions of the regenerate. "There is a sin [*hamartía* (266)] unto death" (1 John 5:16) refers to willful and intentional sin (see also Heb. 10:26, 29) and physical death (Acts 5:1–11; 1 Cor. 5:5; 11:30), and

131   ἁμαρτωλός (268)

there is a sin not unto death. The sins of the regenerate are regrettably unavoidable in view of their present unredeemed body (Rom. 8:2, 3) and the environment in which they live (1 John 2:2). The sinfulness of sin depends on the innate or acquired knowledge of God's expectations (James 4:17).

Syn.: *agnóēma* (51), a sin of ignorance; *opheílēma* ([3783] akin to *opheilē* [3782], a debt), that which is legally due; *adikía* (93), unrighteousness; *adíkēma* (92), a wrong, an injury; *ponēría* (4189), wickedness; *paranomía* (3892), law–breaking; *anomía* (458), lawlessness; *parábasis* (3847), violation, transgression; *kríma* (2917), condemnation; *égklēma* (1462), crime which is tried in court; *sunōmosía* (4945), a plot, conspiracy; *asébeia* (763), impiety, ungodliness; *parakoē* (3876), disobedience; *apeítheia* (543), obstinate rejection of God's will; *paráptōma* (3900), a false step, a blunder; *ptōsis* (4431), a fall; *apostasía* (646), a standing away from, although not necessarily a departure from a position in which one stood; *aitía* (156) and *aítion* (158), a crime, a legal ground for punishment, fault; *hēttēma* (2275), a loss, defeat, defect; *hamártēma* (265), an act of sin or disobedience to divine requirement and expectation.

Ant.: *sōtēría* (4991), salvation; *dikaiosúnē* (1343), righteousness; *áphesis* (859), forgiveness, removal of sin; *cháris* (5485), grace; *hagiōsúnē* (42), the state of holiness; *hagiótes* (41), inherent holiness.

267. ἀμάρτυρος amárturos; gen. *amartúrou*, masc.–fem., neut. *amárturon*, adj. from the priv. *a* (1), without, and *mártus* (3144), a witness. Without a witness (Acts 14:17).

268. ἁμαρτωλός hamartōlós; gen. *hamartōloú*, masc.–fem., neut. *hamartōlón*, adj. from *hamartánō* (264), to deviate, miss the mark, sin. Erring from the way or mark. In the NT, metaphorically used as an adj. or subst.

(I) As adj., erring from the divine law, sinful, wicked, impious.

(A) Generally: a sinful generation (Mark 8:38); a sinful man, a sinner (Luke 5:8; 19:7; 24:7; John 9:16, 24); a sinful woman (Luke 7:37, 39; Sept.: Num. 32:14; Is. 1:4); "more wicked than all others" (a.t.; Luke 13:2); a sinner (Luke 18:13; Rom. 3:7); sinful, sinners (Rom. 5:8; Gal. 2:17; James 4:8).

(B) Oblivious to the consequences of sin, guilty and exposed to punishment: (Rom. 5:19, many became exposed to the punishment of sin; 7:13; Gal. 2:15; Jude 1:15, ungodly persons deserving of punishment).

(II) As subst., a sinner, transgressor, impious person.

(A) Generally (Matt. 9:10, 11, 13; 11:19; Mark 2:15–17; Luke 5:30, 32; 6:32–34; 7:34; 15:1, 2, 7, 10; John 9:25, 31; 1 Tim. 1:9, 15; Heb. 7:26; 12:3; James 5:20; 1 Pet. 4:18; Sept.: Ps. 1:1, 5; 37:12, 20; Is. 13:9; Ezek. 33:8, 19; Amos 9:8).

(B) The Jews called the Gentiles sinners or despisers of God and considered them heathen or pagan, *tá éthnē* (1484), the nations (Matt. 26:45 [cf. Matt. 20:19; Mark 10:33; Luke 18:32; Sept.: Is. 14:5]).

(C) Often connected with *telōnes* (pl. [5077]), publicans or tax collectors (Matt. 9:10, 11; 11:19; Mark 2:15, 16; Luke 7:34; 15:1) who were in bad repute among Jews and Greeks. See also Matt. 26:45; Mark 14:41; Luke 5:30; 6:33, 34; 7:39; 13:2; 15:2, 7, 10; 18:13; 19:7; John 9:16, 24, 25, 31; Rom. 3:7; Gal. 2:15, 17; Heb. 12:3; James 4:8; 5:20; 1 Pet. 4:18.

Syn.: *asebḗs* (765), impious, ungodly; *ápistos* (571), an unbeliever; *opheilétēs* (3781), a debtor; *énochos* (177), guilty of something; *aítios* (159), one to be blamed; *ádikos* (94), unjust.

Ant.: *athōos* (121), innocent; *anaítios* (338), guiltless; *anamártētos* (361), one without sin; *ákakos* (172), one without malice; *díkaios* (1342), just, one who recognizes that God has rights upon his life. He submits himself to be God's rightful possession and, therefore, acquires God's

Since we know *sin* by *hamartia* (a noun) and *hamartano* (a verb), read both of these definitions in Zodhiates' on pages 90-92. Start with the definition in the first paragraph, and then look in the paragraphs that follow (such as I, II, and so on) for your references in 1 John 3 to see more detail on what is meant by *sin* in those verses. Write any information you find out about *sin* on the lines below.

_____

_____

"Uh-oh, hurry up! I think our suspect just headed out the back door. Yep, he's gone. Let's talk to Mr. Madison, our bookstore owner, and see if he can give us some information on where *sin* might be headed next."

Mr. Madison saw *sin* head down one of the side streets. You know *sin* likes to creep around to keep from being exposed. Mr. Madison thinks we should check out the library on Vine Street. Grab Sam's leash and let's go.

"Look, Max, over there next to the reference books. There he is!"

"Shhhhh, Molly, we're in a library. Sam, you have to wait here by the door. Be a good dog, put on your shades, and keep a close watch. We'll be right back."

Let's use *Vine's* dictionary to get more information about sin. To use *Vine's* dictionary, you would look up the word *sin* the same way that you would in a regular dictionary. When you find the word *sin*, look underneath the word and you will see that it is divided into categories: nouns, adjectives, and verbs. Under each category it will have the Greek word for A. the noun (*sin*), B. the adjective (*sin*), and C. the verb (*sin*). Since you have used your concordance, you know which Greek words you are looking for: the noun *hamartia* and the verb *hamartano*. So read these definitions, starting in the first paragraph. Then look for your references in 1 John 3 to see more of what is meant by *sin* in those verses. Use the pages from *Vine's* dictionary on the next page.

Vine's Dictionary

SIM	32	SIN

For SIMPLICITY see LIBERALITY

SIN (Noun and Verb)
A. Nouns.

1. HAMARTIA (ἁμαρτία) is, lit., a missing of the mark, but this etymological meaning is largely lost sight of in the N.T. It is the most comprehensive term for moral obliquity. It is used of sin as (*a*) a principle or source of action, or an inward element producing acts, e.g., Rom. 3 : 9 ; 5 : 12, 13, 20 ; 6 : 1, 2 ; 7 : 7 (abstract for concrete) ; 7 : 8 (twice), 9, 11, 13, " sin, that it might be shewn to be sin," i.e., ' sin became death to me, that it might be exposed in its heinous character : ' in the last clause, " sin might become exceeding sinful," i.e., through the holiness of the Law, the true nature of sin was designed to be manifested to the conscience ;

(*b*) a governing principle or power, e.g., Rom. 6 : 6, " (the body) of sin ", here sin is spoken of as an organized power, acting through the members of the body, though the seat of sin is in the will (the body is the organic instrument) ; in the next clause, and in other passages, as follows, this governing principle is personified, e.g., Rom. 5 : 21 ; 6 : 12, 14, 17 ; 7 : 11, 14, 17, 20, 23, 25 ; 8 : 2 ; 1 Cor. 15 : 56 ; Heb. 3 : 13 ; 11 : 25 ; 12 : 4 ; Jas. 1 : 15 (2nd part) ;

(*c*) a generic term (distinct from specific terms such as No. 2, yet sometimes inclusive of concrete wrong doing, e.g., John 8 : 21, 34, 46 ; 9 : 41 ; 15 : 22, 24 ; 19 : 11) ; in Rom. 8 : 3, " God, sending His own Son in the likeness of sinful flesh," lit., ' flesh of sin,' the flesh stands for the body, the instrument of indwelling sin [Christ, pre-existently the Son of God, assumed human flesh, " of the substance of the Virgin Mary ;" the reality of incarnation was His, without taint of sin (for *homoiōma*, likeness, see LIKENESS)], " and *as an offering* for sin," i.e., ' a sin-offering ' (so the Sept., e.g., in Lev. 4 : 32 ; 5 : 6, 7, 8, 9), " condemned sin in the flesh," i.e., Christ, having taken human nature, sin apart (Heb. 4 : 15), and having lived a sinless life, died under the condemnation and judgment due to our sin ; for the generic sense see further, e.g., Heb. 9 : 26 ; 10 : 6, 8, 18 ; 13 : 11 ; 1 Cor. 15 : 34 (1st part ; in the 2nd part, sin is defined as " lawlessness," R.V.), 8, 9 ; in these verses the A.V. use of the verb to commit is misleading ; not the committal of an act is in view, but a continuous course of sin, as indicated by the R.V., " doeth." The Apostle's use of the present tense of *poieō*, to do, virtually expresses the meaning of *prassō*, to practise, which John does not use (it is not infrequent in this sense in Paul's Epp., e.g., Rom. 1 : 32, R.V. ; 2 : 1 ; Gal. 5 : 21 ; Phil. 4 : 9) ; 1 Pet. 4 : 1 (singular in the best texts), lit., ' has been made to cease from sin,' i.e., as a result of suffering in the flesh, the mortifying of our members, and of obedience to a Saviour who suffered in flesh. Such no longer lives in the flesh, " to the lusts of men, but to the will of God ; " sometimes the word is used as virtually

SIN	33	SIN

equivalent to a condition of sin, e.g., John 1 : 29, " the sin (not sins) of the world ; " 1 Cor. 15 : 17 ; or a course of sin, characterized by continuous acts, e.g., 1 Thess. 2 : 16 ; in 1 John 5 : 16 (2nd part) the R.V. marg., is probably to be preferred, " there is sin unto death," not a special act of sin, but the state or condition producing acts ; in ver. 17, " all unrighteousness is sin " is not a definition of sin (as in 3 : 4), it gives a specification of the term in its generic sense ;

(*d*) a sinful deed, an act of sin, e.g., Matt. 12 : 31 ; Acts 7 : 60 ; Jas. 1 : 15 (1st part) ; 2 : 9 ; 4 : 17 ; 5 : 15, 20 ; 1 John 5 : 16 (1st part).

Notes : (1) Christ is predicated as having been without sin in every respect, e.g., (*a*), (*b*), (*c*) above, 2 Cor. 5 : 21 (1st part) ; 1 John 3 : 5 ; John 14 : 30 ; (*d*) John 8 : 46 ; Heb. 4 : 15 ; 1 Pet. 2 : 22. (2) In Heb. 9 : 28 (2nd part) the reference is to a sin offering. (3) In 2 Cor. 5 : 21, " Him . . . He made to be sin " indicates that God dealt with Him as He must deal with sin, and that Christ fulfilled what was typified in the guilt offering. (4) For the phrase " man of sin " in 2 Thess. 2 : 3, see INIQUITY, No. 1.

2. HAMARTĒMA (ἁμάρτημα), akin to No. 1, denotes an act of disobedience to Divine law [as distinct from No. 1 (*a*), (*b*), (*c*)] ; plural in Mark 3 : 28 ; Rom. 3 : 25 ; 2 Pet. 1 : 9, in some texts ; sing. in Mark 3 : 29 (some mss. have *krisis*, A.V., " damnation ") ; 1 Cor. 6 : 18.¶

Notes : (1) For *paraptōma*, rendered " sins " in the A.V. in Eph. 1 : 7 ; 2 : 5 ; Col. 2 : 13 (R.V., " trespass "), see TRESPASS. In Jas. 5 : 16, the best texts have No. 1 (R.V., " sins "). (2) For synonymous terms see DISOBEDIENCE, ERROR, FAULT, INIQUITY, TRANSGRESSION, UNGODLINESS.

B. Adjective.

ANAMARTĒTOS (ἀναμάρτητος), without sin (*a*, negative, *n*, euphonic, and C, No. 1), is found in John 8 : 7.¶ In the Sept., Deut. 29 : 19.¶

C. Verbs.

1. HAMARTANŌ (ἁμαρτάνω), lit., to miss the mark, is used in the N.T. (*a*) of sinning against God, (1) by angels, 2 Pet. 2 : 4 ; (2) by man, Matt. 27 : 4 ; Luke 15 : 18, 21 (Heaven standing, by metonymy, for God) ; John 5 : 14 ; 8 : 11 ; 9 : 2, 3 ; Rom. 2 : 12 (twice) ; 3 : 23 ; 5 : 12, 14, 16 ; 6 : 15 ; 1 Cor. 7 : 28 (twice), 36 ; 15 : 34 ; Eph. 4 : 26 ; 1 Tim. 5 : 20 ; Tit. 3 : 11 ; Heb. 3 : 17 ; 10 : 26 ; 1 John 1 : 10 ; in 2 : 1 (twice), the aorist tense in each place, referring to an act of sin ; on the contrary, in 3 : 6 (twice), 8, 9, the present tense indicates, not the committal of an act, but the continuous practice of sin [see on A, No. 1 (*c*)], in 5 : 16 (twice) the present tense indicates the condition resulting from an act, " unto death " signifying ' tending towards death ; ' (*b*) against Christ, 1 Cor. 8 : 12 ; (*c*) against man, (1) a brother, Matt. 18 : 15, R.V., " sin " (A.V., " trespass ") ; ver. 21 ; Luke 17 : 3, 4, R.V., " sin " (A.V., " trespass ") ; 1 Cor. 8 : 12 ; (2) in Luke 15 : 18, 21, against the father by the prodigal son, " in thy sight " being suggestive of befitting reverence ; (*d*) against Jewish law, the Temple, and Cæsar, Acts 25 : 8, R.V., " sinned " (A.V.,

SIN	34	SIN

" offended ") ; (*e*) against one's own body, by fornication, 1 Cor. 6 : 18 ; (*f*) against earthly masters by servants, 1 Pet. 2 : 20, R.V., " (when) ye sin (and are buffeted for it)," A.V.," (when ye be buffeted) for your faults," lit., ' having sinned.'¶

2. PROAMARTANŌ (προαμαρτάνω), to sin previously (*pro*, before, and No. 1), occurs in 2 Cor. 12 : 21 ; 13 : 2, R.V. in each place, " have sinned heretofore " (so A.V. in the 2nd ; in the 1st, " have sinned already ").¶

Now write any information you discover about *sin* from *Vine's* on the lines below.

Great detective work!

Our suspect *sin* sure is slippery! While you were hard at work searching the library, he slipped out the door. But I'm sure if you'll ask the librarian she may be able to give us some information on where *sin*'s hideout might be. We need a witness to give us *sin*'s address. Then we'll check out some of those addresses tomorrow.

Eyewitness Account

The librarian had a great idea to help us find some of *sin*'s addresses. She said we should use cross-referencing—that's where you compare Scripture with Scripture. Remember we learned in Week Three that Scripture is the best interpreter of Scripture. We have to check the whole Word of God.

To look for cross-references, you look up *sin* in the concordance that is in the back of your Bible (which only gives a few places it is used) or in your *New American Standard Exhaustive Concordance* to see every place else it is found in the Bible. Then you look up those passages of Scripture to see what else you can learn about *sin* from the other passages. Remember, Scripture never contradicts Scripture.

Now let's see where else *sin* hangs out. Turn to page 81 in this book to our concordance pages and look up *sin* again. Wow! Just look at all those addresses. And there are more in the concordance. We just copied this one page! *Sin* sure shows up a lot in the Bible. It must be pretty important for God to mention it so much.

The librarian has narrowed down some of the addresses for us to look for *sin*. Let's look up the following addresses and make a list on what we learn about *sin*. These are key verses that will give us a good profile on *sin*. We'll know exactly what *sin* is!

1 John 3:4 _____

1 John 5:17 _____

James 4:17 _____

_____

Romans 14:23 _____

John 16:9 _____

Now, Isaiah 53:6 doesn't specifically say WHAT *sin* is, but it shows us WHAT *sin* (iniquity) does, how we sin.

Read Isaiah 53:6 and see what we do that is just like what sheep do.

They go a ___ ___ ___ ___ ___, and each of us has

_____ to _____ _____ _____.

So this verse shows us that the root of all sin, where it begins, is with us. We do what we want to do rather than what God wants us to do. That's why we tell lies, cheat, talk back, disobey our parents, and do lots of other things that are not right in God's eyes. This makes us unrighteous. We do those things because we want our way instead of God's.

Now before we head back to the tree house, we need to apply WHAT we've learned about sin to our lives.

Do "believers" sin? ___ Yes   ___ No

I Did It

My name _____

My address _____
STREET OR P.O. BOX

_____
CITY   STATE   ZIP CODE

My phone number is (___) _____

My address is _____

I am _____ years old.

The study I did was _____ .
(TITLE OF BOOK)

Here's where I bought it _____

My favorite thing about it was _____

_____

I was excited when God showed me _____

Here's the grown-up who knows I d d it: _____

_____
MOM'S OR DAD'S SIGNATURE

I've also done these other Discover 4 Yourself studies _____

_____

Mail this postcard. We have something special we want to send you!

I ACED THE INDUCTIVE DETECTIVE'S EXAM IN *HOW TO STUDY YOUR BIBLE FOR KIDS!*

I scored between 150-200 points. This is my score: _____

This is the grown-up who knows I did it: _____

_____
(Mom's, Dad's, teacher's, or grown-up's signature)

My Name _____

My Address _____

City _____

State _____ Zip Code _____

My phone number (___) _____

I am _____ years old.

Please send me an excerpt from the *New Inductive Study Bible* and a special surprise for completing this study and acing the Inductive Detective's Exam!

BUSINESS REPLY MAIL

FIRST-CLASS MAIL PERMIT NO. 48 CHATTANOOGA TN

POSTAGE WILL BE PAID BY ADDRESSEE

PRECEPT MINISTRIES
P O BOX 182218
CHATTANOOGA TN 37422-9901

NO POSTAGE
NECESSARY
IF MAILED
IN THE
UNITED STATES

BUSINESS REPLY MAIL

FIRST-CLASS MAIL PERMIT NO. 48 CHATTANOOGA TN

POSTAGE WILL BE PAID BY ADDRESSEE

PRECEPT MINISTRIES
P O BOX 182218
CHATTANOOGA TN 37422-9901

WHAT verse shows this? 1 John 2:_____

Do real believers, children of God, sin continuously, as a habit of their life? ___ Yes　___ No

WHAT verses in 1 John 3:4-10 show this? Go back to page 84 and look at the verses with their tenses. List below every verse number and the words that prove that a child of God, one who abides in Jesus, cannot practice sin. We will give you lots of lines to write on, but you don't have to use them all.

_____

_____

_____

_____

_____

WHAT do children of God practice?

r _ _ _ _ _ _ _ _ _ _ _ _

Children of God also l _ _ _ their brothers (other Christians).

WHEN you or a Christian sins, WHAT should you do? (Look up 1 John 1:9.)

_____

WHAT does God do? (Look at 1 John 1:9 again.)

_____

_____

Now what about the person we mentioned at the beginning of this week—the guy who said he was a Christian but whose deeds are bad? Remember, he was sinning just like he did before he said he became a Christian, and he doesn't love other Christians. Have you got your answer? Is he a child of God or a child of the devil?

And HOW would you tell him to move from the devil's family to God's?

_____

If you think *you* are a real Christian, HOW can you tell?

_____

Did you learn your memory verse this week? Try saying it to a friend or a grown-up.

Well, you did it! You completed another week. That's impressive! You are learning how to get at the meaning of something through correct interpretation. Congratulations.

Only two more cases and you'll have your inductive detective's card. Hang in there, friend. You can do it! We are so proud of you!

5

Historical and Cultural Context: The Case of the Missing Soldier

"Hey, Max, what happened to that file I had on soldiers? I put it in this drawer, and now I can't find it."

"Let me see, Molly. Look in that box over by the window. I was looking at the file before I went home last night, and I think I put it in that box."

Many times a detective will review his old case files as he tries to solve a new case. This week our investigation of "The Case of the Missing Soldier" will help us see the importance of understanding the times in which a book of the Bible was written.

Get the History! Look at the Culture!

Max and Molly have been asked to find the missing soldier. To do this, they need to do some investigating and get some background material on soldiers. Your assignment, inductive detectives, is to help them. If you remember, Max and Molly explained a little bit about historical context in Week One. Historical context helps us understand the meaning of Scripture by looking at the time in history when an event happens. For instance, did it happen in Old Testament times or New Testament times? What was going on in the world at that time? Knowing this, along with cultural context, helps you interpret the Bible accurately.

Knowing the cultural context helps you understand how people lived in a particular period of history. Different nations have different customs—different ways they live and do things. This is their culture. If you went to India, Russia, Japan, China, or Africa to serve the Lord as a missionary, like the apostle Paul and other great men and women have, you would find that each country has its own culture. Therefore, you would want to know about their culture before you went. It would also help you understand the history of their country.

This week we are going to see how we can discover the historical and cultural context of books of the Bible.

What do you think soldiers were like in Bible times? Did they have guns and automatic weapons? How did they defend themselves?

"Come here, Sam, ol' boy. Let's begin our investigation." Inductive detectives, let's turn to page 182 to our Observation Worksheet on John 18. Read John 18:1-14 and mark *Roman cohort, officers,* and *commander* with a sword like this:

Don't forget to mark any reference to WHERE by double underlining what tells you "where" in green. Mark any references to WHEN by drawing a green clock like this:

Then tomorrow we will interrogate this text.

When you finish reading and marking John 18, look at the soldier's shield on the next page and solve the mystery of your memory verse.

You can break the code by crossing out every third letter and writing the letters that are left (the ones that aren't crossed out) in the blanks below. These verses are found in Ephesians 6, verses _____ and _____.

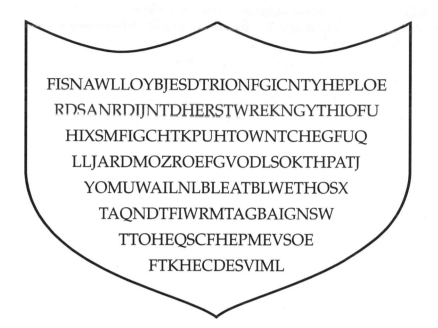

FISNAWLLOYBJESDTRIONFGICNTYHEPLOE
RDSANRDIJNTDHERSTWREKNGYTHIOFU
HIXSMFIGCHTKPUHTOWNTCHEGFUQ
LLJARDMOZROEFGVODLSOKTHPATJ
YOMUWAILNLBLEATBLWETHOSX
TAQNDTFIWRMTAGBAIGNSW
TTOHEQSCFHEPMEVSOE
FTKHECDESVIML

——————————, —— ——————————

—— ——— ————————— ——— ——

——— ————————— ——

——— ——————. ———— ——

——— ————— ————— —

—— ————, —— —————

——— ————— —— —————

————— ————— ————————

——— ——————— ——

——— —————.

Ephesians 6:___-___

Great decoding. Now open your Bible and read from Ephesians 6:10 on until you discover the "address" of the verses you are to memorize. Now practice your memory verses by saying them out loud three times, three times each day. Try to do it when you get out of bed, when you eat lunch, and just before you go to bed.

Let's Investigate

"Hey, Max, I have a great idea. Let's reenact the scene in John 18 with the Roman cohorts. You know how detectives on television often act out what happened in order to help them solve their cases."

"That's a great idea, Molly, but first we should make sure we have the information we need to act out the scene. We need to find out about these Roman cohorts."

Now, inductive detectives, first things first. How do soldiers know what to do? Where do they get their orders? Soldiers get their orders from their commanding officer. So, just like a soldier, we need to check in with our Commander-in-chief. Of course, you know that's God! So pray, ask God to show you what kind of Christian soldier you are, and then report to duty.

Our first order of the day is to head back to the garden in John 18 and get an eyewitness account on what's happening. Turn to page 182 to John 18. Someone is about to be arrested, and we need to find out WHO. WHERE is this happening? WHEN? WHERE was He going to be taken? The answers to these questions will give us the historical context. Keep your eyes open, inductive detectives. Get the answers you need by interrogating the text. Remember to give it the 5 W's and an H! Then find the answers in the word search on page 105.

John 18:1 To WHOM is Jesus speaking?

His ~~Father~~ disciples

John 18:1 WHERE did Jesus go?

~~Kidron Valley~~ Garden

John 18:2 WHO betrayed Jesus?

Judas ✓

John 18:3 WHOM did Judas receive from the chief priests and the Pharisees?

~~Roman~~ Cohort and officers
~~soldiers~~ ~~officials~~

John 18:3 WHAT did the Roman cohort come with?

lanterns, torches, and __weapons__ ✓

John 18:3 WHEN was Jesus arrested—WHAT time of day? (Your clue to the time is in what the cohorts are carrying.)

_____ morning   _____ noon   __✓__ night

John 18:5 For WHOM were the Roman cohort looking?

Jesus ✓

John 18:6 WHAT happened to the Roman cohort when Jesus said, "I am He"?

They ___fell___ to the ground.

John 18:8-9 WHY did Jesus tell the cohort to let His disciples go their way?

to ___fulfill___ the word which He spoke

John 18:10 WHO cut off the high priest's slave's ear?

Simon   Peter
_____

John 18:10 HOW did he cut off the ear?

_____

John 18:11 WHAT did Jesus tell Peter to do with the sword?

put it into the _____

John 18:12 WHAT did the Roman cohort, the commander, and the officers of the Jews do to Jesus?

_____

John 18:13 WHERE did they take Jesus first?

_____

John 18:14 WHO said that it is expedient for one man to die for many?

_____

Now, look for the words you wrote in each blank in the word search on the next page and circle each one.

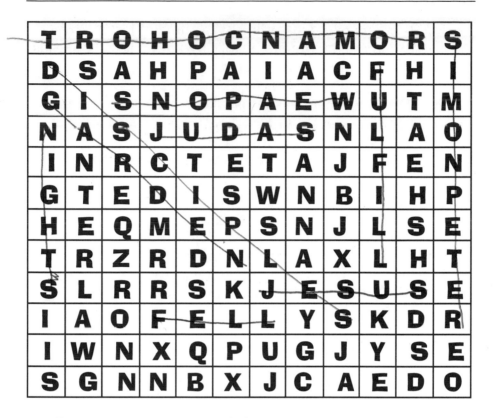

T	R	O	H	O	C	N	A	M	O	R	S
D	S	A	H	P	A	I	A	C	F	H	I
G	I	S	N	O	P	A	E	W	U	T	M
N	A	S	J	U	D	A	S	N	L	A	O
I	N	R	C	T	E	T	A	J	F	E	N
G	T	E	D	I	S	W	N	B	I	H	P
H	E	Q	M	E	P	S	N	J	L	S	E
T	R	Z	R	D	N	L	A	X	L	H	T
S	L	R	R	S	K	J	E	S	U	S	E
I	A	O	F	E	L	L	Y	S	K	D	R
I	W	N	X	Q	P	U	G	J	Y	S	E
S	G	N	N	B	X	J	C	A	E	D	O

Great interrogation! Don't forget to practice your memory verse!

Putting Together All the Clues

"Wow, Max, I never realized how knowing WHO arrested Jesus, and WHERE He was taken would help us know WHAT time in history it happened."

"That's right, Molly. Those WHO and WHERE questions are clues to understanding the historical context in John 18."

WHAT kind of cohort arrested Jesus? __ __ __ __ __
Unscramble the answer. (NAORM)

This tells you who was ruling at the time of Jesus' arrest. We can also know the time in history by knowing WHO Jesus was taken to when He was arrested.

To WHAT four men was Jesus taken?

> The first answer is in this chapter of John.
> It was __ __ __ __ __ (NNASA), the father-in-law of the second man.
>
> The second man is __ __ __ __ __ __ __ __ (AIPACHAS). Jesus spent the night there.
>
> The third man is found by doing a cross-reference. Read Matthew 27:1-2. His name was __ __ __ __ __ __ (LAIPTE).
>
> The fourth man is mentioned in Luke 23:6-7. His name is __ __ __ __ __ (DEROH). From there Jesus was taken back to the third man, whose name you just figured out.
> Write it out again for review! _____

Wow! You have just uncovered some important historical information. You know what the high priest's name was, the governor's name, and the name of the man who was ruling for Rome over the Jews—the man who considered himself the king of the Jews (Mark 6:14).

WHAT else can we discover by looking at the historical context and the cultural context? Did Roman soldiers carry guns like our soldiers or policeman do today? ___ Yes ___ No

HOW do you know this?

WHAT weapon did Peter use to cut off the slave's ear?

_____

Let's do some cross-referencing. Look up and read Matthew 26:47-52.

WHAT did the multitude carry in verse 47?

__ __ __ __ __ __ (SSOWRD) and

__ __ __ __ __ (BCULS)

Do we carry swords around today? No, we live in a different time and a different culture.

Another way to look for clues about historical and cultural context is to go to a Bible dictionary or a book on manners and customs of Bible times. Books like these were written to help you understand what things meant during Bible times such as the importance of washing people's feet. Do you wash people's feet when they come to your house for dinner? No, but they did during Bible times and by understanding the custom (cultural context) of washing feet you can understand the special significance of Jesus washing His disciples' feet in John 13. So you see there are a lot of different cultural things to learn on many different subjects.

To learn more about Roman armies Molly and Max used a book called *The New Manners and Customs of Bible Times* by Ralph Gower.

To investigate Roman armies, you need to go to the back of that book to the index and look up any word that will help you find information on the Roman soldiers such as: Roman army, soldiers, or armies. Then you turn to the pages that it lists as having information about this subject and read the information to find out about the time of history and the customs (cultural context) at the time.

Look at the sketch of the Roman soldier below to see WHAT Roman soldiers looked liked, and WHAT Roman soldiers wore. This will be very helpful as we look at the cultural context tomorrow. Maybe it will help us solve the case of the missing Christian soldier.

Molly, Max, and Sam are going to get some of their friends to help them reenact the scene in the garden with the Roman cohort. Why don't you ask your mom and dad or some of your friends to help you reenact it also. Get someone to be Jesus, Judas, Peter, one of the Roman soldiers, and the slave Malchus. Use the facts you've uncovered to get the historical context right, such as making a paper torch and coloring it red or using a lantern instead of a flashlight. Cut a sword out of cardboard. Be creative and have fun! And think of what your friends and family are going to learn from the Bible. Exciting!

A Good Soldier

"Sam, where are you? Come here, boy. Come on, Sam, where are you? Hey, Molly, did you see Sam on your way over here?"

"No, Max, I didn't. Maybe he's out behind the fence. You know how he loves to sniff out clues."

"You're right, Molly. Sam always comes when I call him unless he's found something interesting. We better try to find him."

Molly and Max dashed across the yard and out the gate. "Sam, there you are! What have you got there? Look, Molly, Sam's found a chopstick."

Sam's tail was wagging like a flag on the Fourth of July as he tossed his head in Max's direction, showing off his find.

"Sam, did you dig that out of Mrs. Dean's trash can? Mrs. Dean must have had Chinese food last night."

"Great deduction, Sherlock."

"Okay, Molly, give me a break. But we are going to look at cultural context today with our inductive detectives. This is a great way to show them how knowing the culture helps us better understand what something means. For instance, in China we know the people eat with chopsticks instead of forks. Chopsticks are a part of the Chinese culture."

"You're right, Max. Let's race back to the tree house and see what we can learn about cultural context and soldiers."

Before he was executed by the Roman government because of his Christian testimony, the apostle Paul wrote a letter to Timothy. Paul was Timothy's "father in the Lord," which means that Paul introduced Timothy to Jesus Christ and Timothy became a believer. Timothy was a real child of God. His deeds proved it.

Because this was Paul's last letter to his son, it contains a lot of important information. Paul wanted the very best for "his son, Timothy." That's why he wrote him this letter. Don't you think Timothy probably read it often after Paul's death?

Let's begin our investigation by reading 2 Timothy 2:1-4 printed out below. Mark every reference to Timothy in orange. Don't forget the pronouns!

> *You therefore, my son, be strong in the grace that is in Christ Jesus. The things which you have heard from me in the presence of many witnesses, entrust these to faithful men who will be able to teach others also. Suffer hardship with me, as a good soldier of Christ Jesus. No soldier in active service entangles himself in the affairs of everyday life, so that he may please the one who enlisted him as a soldier.*

Hey, did you notice the word *soldier*? Great. Now go back and read 2 Timothy 2:1-4 again. This time mark every reference to a soldier like this: ✗ (don't forget to mark the pronouns *he* and *him* that refer to a soldier).

WHY does Paul use a soldier as an example in his letter to Timothy? It's because soldiers were important in New Testament times. The Roman Empire ruled over most of the world at that time. And it was the Roman soldiers who helped to keep law and order. Timothy would know exactly what Paul was talking about when he used the soldier as an example. Therefore, we want to look at the cultural context of what Paul is telling Timothy.

WHAT were Roman soldiers like? HOW did they behave? HOW well trained were they? WHAT was their uniform? WHAT were their weapons? These are some of the questions we want to find the answers to. So, like a good inductive detective, interrogate the text and see what you can learn about soldiers in the days when Paul wrote to Timothy, which was about A.D. 64.

List everything you observe about a soldier on the lines below. Next to each thing you see, write the verse number that you saw it in.

_____

_____

_____

_____

_____

_____

_____

_____

Once detectives get their information, they often get a sketch drawn of a suspect to help them find the person they are looking for. Connect the dots and see what Paul was "sketching" for Timothy.

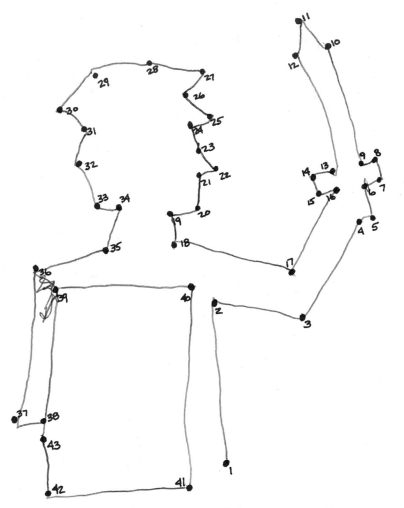

Now let's solve the mystery of the missing Christian soldier. There are a lot of AWOL Christian soldiers these days.

AWOL is a military term used to describe a soldier who is "absent without leave." In other words, the soldier is not on duty where he belongs! Paul called it "active service." Let's read 2 Timothy 2:3-4 again. This time underline *active service*. When we underline things, it often emphasizes their importance.

Suffer hardship with me, as a good soldier of Christ Jesus. No soldier in active service entangles himself in the affairs of everyday life, so that he may please the one who enlisted him as a soldier.

When a Roman soldier was off duty, his belt that carried his sword in its sheath hung loose on his body. When he was in active service, his belt was tight. He was fully dressed— ready for battle! His sword was at hand.

Also, he wasn't so busy with his own affairs and interests that he forgot he was enlisted in an army. If he was a good soldier, he was a soldier all the way. He didn't entangle himself, tie himself up in "civilian" things that distracted him from his duties or kept him so busy that he didn't have time for training as a soldier. First and foremost, he was a soldier who had one purpose, one goal, one passion, and that was to please his commander-in-chief.

Now HOW does this apply to you? To all Christians? It means that once we become a Christian, we are enlisted by God into His army. Our goal, our passion, our purpose should be to please God, our Commander-in-chief above *all* others. And we are to do this even when it's hard. Maybe other kids or even adults will tease us or put us down because we are really dedicated Christians who are going to study our Bibles, go to church, and go on mission trips to places that are hard to live in. But that is not to stop us. We are to please God. He's to always come before our friends.

So what is the mystery of the missing Christian soldier? It is those who say they love Jesus but forget they are called to be good soldiers no matter how hard it gets. The Bible says, "There's no retirement in the time of war." Until Jesus comes and rules over this earth and brings us with Him, we are to be on active duty.

If you find any missing Christian soldiers, remind them of this!

Another case is solved, but our work for this week is not done.

Tomorrow we need to talk about going to war against the devil!

The Armor of God

"Molly, do you know how soldiers get ready for battle?"

"Sure, Max. They spend lots of time training, exercising, learning how to use their weapons, and planning their strategy."

"Right! It's important for us to understand how the soldier's weapons were used in Bible times, since Paul uses a custom (putting on the armor) to help show the Ephesians how to stand strong in the Lord."

Okay, inductive detectives, are you ready for your last training exercise dealing with cultural context? Turn to page 169 to your Observation Worksheet on Ephesians 6 and read verses 10-18. As you read, there is a very important command you don't want to miss: *Put on the full armor of God,* so put a big circle around that phrase. Let's also mark the phrase *stand firm* by putting a box around it.

Now let's investigate WHAT Paul tells them to do.

Ephesians 6:10 WHAT were they to be strong in?

_____

Ephesians 6:11 WHAT were they to put on?

_____

Ephesians 6:12 WHO is our struggle as Christians against?

It's not against_____

But

against: 1. _____

against: 2. _____

against: 3. _____

against: 4. _____

Let's stop here for a moment and think about what we just saw. WHO do you think rules over all those that we struggle against? Look at verse 11, and you'll see who heads up that army! Write out his name:_____

Now go back and put a red pitchfork over his name in verse 11.

If our warfare is against the devil and his wicked forces, can we win the battle, the war? ___ Yes ___ No

WHAT are we to do?

Ephesians 6:13 HOW are we to stand?

_____

Ephesians 6:14 WHAT are you to gird your loins with?

_____

Ephesians 6:14 WHAT kind of breastplate are you to put on?

_____

Ephesians 6:15 WHAT are you to put on your feet?

_____

Ephesians 6:16 WHAT kind of shield do you put on?

_____

WHAT does the shield do?

_____

Ephesians 6:17 WHAT is the helmet?

_____

Now stop and think. What kind of a soldier is he describing—an American one, a Canadian one, a German one? No, none of these. WHAT was the cultural context? WHO was ruling then?

WHAT kind of a soldier wore these things?

___ _____ soldier

And WHAT is our weapon when we are dressed in the armor of God (Ephesians 6:17)? Unscramble the answer.

__ __ __ __ __ (owsdr) of the __ __ __ __ __ __ (tpiriS)

And WHAT is that? WHAT is the mystery of the sword? It is the __ __ __ __ (oWrd) of __ __ __ (Gdo).

Now read Ephesians 6:18.

WHAT are we to do at all times?

_____

(In modern-day warfare, that would be using your heavenly cell phone. You've been using that for five weeks now, haven't you?)

To remember to stand firm, we need to have our armor on. So let's practice by drawing each piece of the armor of God and looking at what it represents and how we are to use it.

Draw a soldier in the box below. Now add each piece of armor as we come to it.

1. Soldiers used a belt around their waist to gird their loins. Draw the belt of truth on your soldier. How can you put on the belt of truth? By studying God's Word every day, just like you are doing right now. We are so proud of you. Remember: God's Word, the Bible, is pure truth!

2. Draw the breastplate of righteousness. Soldiers wore the breastplate to protect their vital organs like their heart, lungs, stomach, and kidneys so the enemy's arrows could not get through and kill them. Protect yourself with the breastplate of righteousness. God always does the right thing, and that's what He wants us to do. We can do the right thing by staying away from sin and doing what God says in His Word. Then the enemy can't touch us!

3. Draw some sandals on your soldier's feet to represent the gospel of peace. In Roman times the sandals weren't slick on the bottom; they had "grippers" so the soldier could stand firm and not be shaken. When you know that you belong to God, then there is a peace in your heart. You are on God's side and He's on yours, and the devil can't win against God!

4. Draw the shield of faith. This shield enabled the soldier to put out the flaming arrows that were shot at him. The shield was made of leather and soaked in water so when those fiery missiles came at him, they would sizzle out when they hit the shield. Whenever the enemy throws a lie or a doubt or an accusation at you, just hold up the Word and say, "But God says…" and then give the devil a verse that counteracts the lie. Remember, this is the way Jesus won against the devil when He was tempted in the wilderness. He just said, "But God says…" Make your shield of faith big! The more you know God's Word, the stronger your shield will be. Learn the truth and soak in the water of God's Word every day, and the enemy won't get to you.

5. Draw the helmet of salvation. Soldiers wore this on their head to protect their head from deadly blows. We need to protect our minds by remembering to whom we belong. Christ lives inside of Christians, and He is stronger than the enemy. Greater is He who is in you than he (the devil and his cohorts) who is in the world. Keep your helmet on!

6. Draw the sword of the Spirit. The sword of the Spirit is God's Word. It's our only offensive weapon because it is all we need for victory. The only way we can fight is with God's Word. Pull that sword out of its sheath and use it!

That was a great investigation. Now HOW does it apply to you?

> Do you know how to stand against the devil?
> ___ Yes ___ No

> Are you going to continue to put on the belt of truth and keep it tight? ___ Yes ___ No

The Discover 4 Yourself Inductive Study Series will help you do that. So don't stop with this study. This is just the beginning. You will love the other studies.

> Have you accepted Jesus as your Savior? Do you wear the helmet of salvation? ___ Yes ___ No

> Do you wear the breastplate of righteousness? Are you living for Jesus or for yourself? Do your deeds show you belong to God? Do you practice righteousness and confess your sins when you fail to obey God?
> ___ Yes ___ No

> Have you put on the shoes of the gospel of peace? Do you tell other people about Jesus? ___ Yes ___ No

> Do you carry the shield of faith? Is your trust in the Lord? Do you turn to Him when bad things happen?
> ___ Yes ___ No

> Do you carry the sword of the Spirit? Do you know the Word of God? When people tell lies about God, about His Word, about how we are to live, can you combat these with the Word of God? Can you wield that sword like a mighty soldier? ___ Yes ___ No

Do you pray? Do you keep in touch with the Commander-in-chief, getting His orders, carrying them out, and letting Him know how you are doing and what you need to be a more effective soldier on active duty? ___ Yes ___ No

The only way we can be strong and stand firm is to put on the full armor of God. And it all centers on the Word of God. That's why you are doing a great work! We are proud of you for sharpening your sword by learning how to study God's Word inductively. Remember, it's the only weapon you will ever need.

Tomorrow we start our final case that will complete your detective training and bring you an inductive detective training carrying card when you fill out the card in the back of this book and send it in.

Molly and Max have a fun idea that you might like to try since we have been studying historical and cultural context this week. Let's make a time capsule.

Gather up a few items that show what your culture is like and place them in a sealed container. Choose things like a newspaper, a popular toy, a photograph, a stamp, baseball cards, a CD, etc.

Then dig a hole in your backyard (ask permission first) and bury your container. If you don't want to bury it, place your container on a shelf in the back of your closet.

Decide when you want to dig it up (a year or longer) and see how things have changed since you made your capsule.

6

Search Warrants

Did you know that a detective cannot enter a suspect's house to look for evidence unless he has a search warrant? A search warrant is a written statement on a piece of paper issued by a judge. The detective takes this paper to the suspect. The search warrant gives the detective permission to search the house to look for the evidence he needs to crack his case.

Get those search warrants ready, inductive detectives, as we investigate our final case.

Book Charts, Chapter Themes, and Titles— The Search Begins

"Molly, guess what I saw back in the woods?"

"What, Max?"

"It looks like a fort. Let's write out a search warrant and go look for evidence!"

"That's a great idea, Max. I'll put Sam on his leash. We don't want him to get there before us. He's going to love this! Let's go!"

Okay, inductive detectives, let's get our search warrants ready. We're going to need them as we search for evidence this week in the Gospel of John.

If a person wants to search for God with all his or her heart, then he or she needs to go to God to get a search warrant. And of course, by now you know how to do that—you pray! You ask God for His help searching out His truth so you can know it and live by it. So stop and pray right now. Then we'll  be ready to begin our investigation, learning how to make a book chart on a book of the Bible.

Book charts are very important, and it really is quite a grown-up thing to do. But we believe that because you want to be a fully qualified inductive detective, you are willing to learn how. And like a good soldier, you are willing to discipline yourself for the sake of being a godly young person.

A book chart is a way to record all the important themes that you discover as you study the Bible book by book. After you make a book chart, you are able to review the entire book with just a glance. Or to put it another way, it will help you search out what is in each book very quickly and know exactly what chapter everything is in.

How do you do this?

You study a book of the Bible chapter by chapter, just as we teach you in the Discover 4 Yourself Inductive Series. As you read each chapter in a book of the Bible, you ask yourself the 5 W's and an H questions and look for key repeated words.

The answers to the 5 W's and an H and key words help you see the subject of a chapter—what the chapter is about. The subjects will show the theme of the book. By the theme of the book, we mean what the book as a whole is about.

key words

↓

subjects of chapters

↓

theme of the book

To make a book chart we will look for the main thing that each chapter in the book is about, and then we will make a chapter title up about that theme.

A chapter title should:
1. be as short as possible
2. describe the main thing the chapter is about
3. if possible, use words you find in the chapter instead of your own words
4. be easy to remember
5. be different than the other chapter titles so you can tell one chapter from another.

We will use the Gospel of John to show you how to do this. Remember what we learned in Week Two when we looked at themes for the book of Titus? The Gospel of John has 21 chapters, but since we only have five days, we will do the first four chapters in John for our book chart. We have chosen the Gospel of John because many of you have done *Jesus in the Spotlight* or you are going to do it. This will fit right in with our Discover 4 Yourself Inductive Series.

Because the first chapter of John is so long, we are going to show you what we put down as the theme of chapter 1 and WHY we did it. Then you can begin with chapter 2 tomorrow.

So, inductive detectives, pull out those search warrants. It's time to search the Word. Turn to the book of John on page 171. Read John 1:1 and John 1:14 and mark the key word, *Word*, like this: (draw it blue and color it green). Then answer the following questions about the Word.

1. John 1:1 WHO is the Word?

   The Word was ___God___ .

2. WHERE was the Word?

   The Word was with __God__.

3. WHEN was the Word there?

   in the __beginning__

4. John 1:14 WHAT did the Word become?

   The Word became __flesh__.

5. WHERE did the Word dwell (*dwell* means "live")?

   The Word dwelt among __us__.

6. WHAT did we behold?

   We beheld His __glory__.

7. His glory was as of the only __begotten__
   from the Father, full of grace and truth.

8. Now WHAT is His name? Look at John 1:17.

   __Jesus__ __Christ__

9. And WHAT is Jesus' relationship to God?
   Look at John 1:34.

   He is the __Son__ of God.

If you were to read through the rest of chapter 1 and color every reference to the Word, who is Jesus Christ, you would learn so much about Him. But you can do that when you do *Jesus in the Spotlight*. By the way, since Jesus is the Word why don't you add a cross to your symbol—like this:

So WHAT is the main subject of John chapter 1? You could write it out several ways. We will list some for you, then you choose your favorite and write it on the book chart, "John at a Glance," on page 137. You will write it on the line where the chapter number 1 is.

Possible titles for John 1:
1. The Word Becomes Flesh
2. The Word, Jesus Christ, Becomes Flesh
3. The Word, Jesus the Son of God, Dwells with Men

Did you notice that every title has the word *Word*? That is because it is an important word that describes Jesus and shows us that He was in the beginning with God, that He is God and the Son of God. They saw His glory—it was just like His Father's.

Did you notice that our titles are short and use words that are found in John chapter 1? They show us the main point of this chapter as John opens his Gospel by introducing us to his subject: Jesus Christ, who is the Son of God and who alone can give us eternal life for He is the Lamb of God that takes away the sin of the world (John 1:29).

Isn't that wonderful news? Just think: Jesus can take away your sins and give you eternal life when you believe what the Word of God, the Bible, says about Him.

This has been a great day, hasn't it? We're excited about tomorrow. Get some good rest and think about what you have just learned. Thank God for sending His Son, Jesus Christ, to earth to take away your sins and ours.

Uncovering the Evidence

We're glad you're back. Guess what our detective dog has been doing? Sam has been busy sniffing out clues. While we were sleeping, Sam was on the trail, searching all the way through the Gospel of John, looking to see if God told us exactly WHY this Gospel was written. His sniffin' and searching led him to another secret coded message. Once it has been decoded using the answer key, you will know WHY God had the apostle John write this Gospel a number of years after the other three Gospels—Matthew, Mark, and Luke—were written.

    This is a very important clue that helps us understand WHY John records what he does. So decode it and memorize it. By now you know how to do it 3 x 3 out loud!

Here's the secret message:

YFG   GSVHV   SZEV   YVVM   DIRGGVM   HL
BUT   _THESE_   _HAVE_   _BEEN_   _WRITTEN_   _SO_

GSZG   BLF   NZB   YVORVEV   GSZG   QVHFH   RH
THAT   _YOU_   _MAY_   _BELIEVE_   _THAT_   _JESUS_ _IS_

GSV   XSIRHG,   GSV   HLM   LU   TLW;   ZMW
THE   _CHRIST_,   _THE_   _SON_   _OF_   _GOD_; _AND_

GSZG   YVORVERMT   BLF   NZB   SZEV   ORUV
THAT   _BELIEVING_   _YOU_   _MAY_   _HAVE_   _LIVE_

RM   SRH   MZNV.
_IN_   _HIS_   _NAME_.

QLSM 20:31
JOHN 20:31

Answer Key:

A	B	C	D	E	F	G	H	I
Z	Y	X	W	V	U	T	S	R

J	K	L	M	N	O	P	Q	
Q	P	O	N	M	L	K	J	

R	S	T	U	V	W	X	Y	Z
I	H	G	F	E	D	C	B	A

Now let's analyze what Sam sniffed out. WHAT does this verse clue us into? Let's ask some questions and see what the answers tell us. You know a good detective asks lots of questions.

WHY did John write what he did in this Gospel? WHAT did he want us to believe? Look at the two *thats* and answer the question.

a. *that* Jesus is the C h r i s t (hirtsC) the S o n (Sno) of G o d (oGd)

b. *that* believing we might have _ _ _ _ (flie) in His n a m e (mnea)

Look up and read John 20:30. WHAT did John record that would help us believe this?

John 20:30 _ _ _ _ _ (ingss)

Did John record all of *these* that Jesus did? _ Yes _ No

WHERE were *these* done?

in the presence of His _ _ _ _ _ _ _ _ _ (lscdipies)

Well, Sam has done his job and he's dog-tired, so let's give him a rest and see what we can discover as we search out the theme of John 2.

Let's get started. Turn to your Observation Worksheet on John 2 on page 174. As a result of Sam's search, we want to watch for and mark the following key words:

temple

signs

believe (color it blue)

Double underline in green anything that tells you <u>WHERE</u> Jesus went or WHERE something happened.

John 2:1-2 WHAT event was Jesus invited to?

_____

John 2:3 WHAT happened at this event?

_____

John 2:6-11 WHAT sign did Jesus do?

_____

John 2:13-14 WHERE did Jesus go when He went to Jerusalem?

_____

John 2:15 WHAT did Jesus do?

_____

When they asked Jesus what sign He would do to support why He cast the moneychangers out of the temple, He actually told them the last sign He would do. They didn't understand it, but He told them. He told them He would be raised from the dead after three days: "Destroy this temple [He was referring to His body] and in three days I will raise it up."

Now put on your thinking caps. WHAT does John 2:11 tell you about turning water into wine—what sign was it?

It was the b_____ of Jesus' signs.

And WHAT would His last sign be? His resurrection from the dead! So John 2 tells you of the very first sign Jesus did and the very last sign He did. Isn't that awesome!

John 2:23 Did any believe in Jesus' name? ___ Yes ___ No
   WHY or WHY NOT?

_____

_____

Now think carefully.
   WHAT are the two main things in John 2?

   1. the w_____ at Cana

   2. cleansing the t_____

Now turn to page 137 and write out a title for John 2 and record it on your book chart.

Whew! That was a lot of work. Are you dog-tired like Sam? Well, like Sam you have done a great job. Just think—you are almost ready to finish your inductive detective training.

Bag It and Tag It!

"There he goes, Max. Follow him. Sam is hot on the trail once again, sniffing out clues."

"Molly, grab a baggie. I think Sam's onto something."

When a detective finds a piece of evidence, he puts it in a bag and then he puts a tag on it. This is to protect his evidence. The detective has to be careful not to mess up any fingerprints that may prove who committed the crime. He uses this evidence to help him solve his case and to prove it in court. So as you continue your search of John, be sure to keep your eyes open for the evidence we need to uncover the theme for our book chart. Then, just like a detective, bag it and tag it!

Now talk to "Central Headquarters" and turn to page 176 to begin your search of John 3. Read it and answer the following questions to help us bag the evidence we need to help solve our case.

John 3:1-2 WHO came to see Jesus at night?

_____

John 3:3 WHAT did Jesus tell Nicodemus?

"Unless one is _____ _____ he cannot see

the _____ of _____."

John 3:5-8 WHAT does Jesus explain to Nicodemus in these verses?

Unless one is born of _____ and the _____ he

cannot enter WHERE? the _____ of _____

John 3:6 The first time we are born we are born of flesh. Being born again means we are born of WHAT?

_____

John 3:14-15 WHY must the Son of Man be lifted up?

_____

John 3:16 WHAT did God give the world to show His awesome love?

_____

John 3:16 WHAT happens if you believe in Jesus?

_____

_____

_____

John 3:17 WHY did God send Jesus into the world?

_____

Now, inductive detectives, look on the next page at the path. In order to get to the kingdom of God there is only one way. Start at the beginning of the path, because we are all born of the flesh. Then find your way, using what you have learned in chapter 3, to lead you to the kingdom of God.

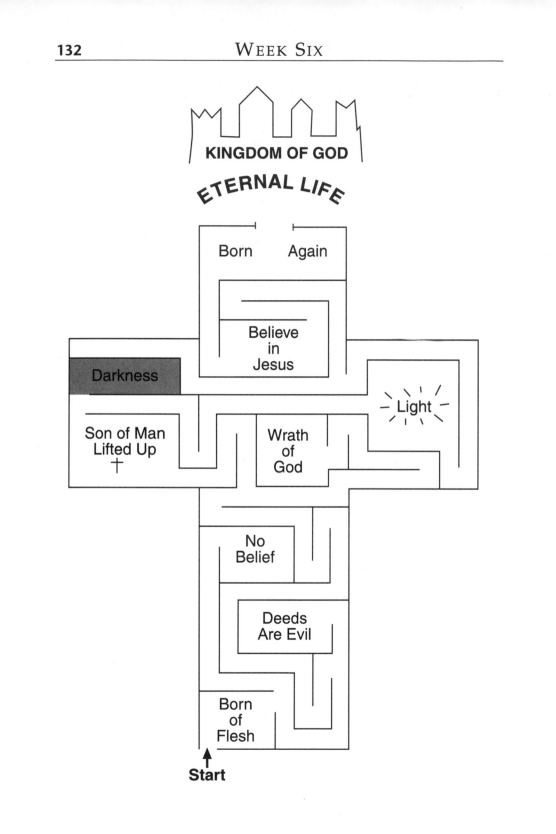

KINGDOM OF GOD

ETERNAL LIFE

Born   Again

Believe
in
Jesus

Darkness

Light

Son of Man
Lifted Up
✝

Wrath
of
God

No
Belief

Deeds
Are Evil

Born
of
Flesh

Start

WHAT is the main thing in John 3?

Being b ___ ___ ___ a ___ ___ ___ ___, believing in
Jesus Christ and receiving eternal life.

Now bag the evidence, turn to page 137, and write your
title for John 3 on your book chart.

Witnesses

"Hey, Molly, we have discovered some awesome evidence.
Now all we need are some witnesses."

"Let's keep our eyes and ears open, Max. I'm sure we can
find someone who saw what happened."

Finding a witness can be very important to a detective.
The witness can help him prove his case by telling what he or
she has seen or heard.

Today as we search for the theme of John 4 for our book
chart, keep a close eye out for witnesses to help you in your
search.

Now turn to page 178 to begin your search on John 4.
Read it and mark the following key words:

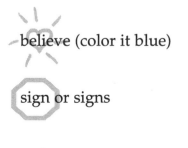 believe (color it blue)

woman

sign or signs

worship

water

John 4:4-5 WHAT city did Jesus pass through on His way to Galilee?

_____

John 4:5-6 WHY did Jesus stop there?

He was _____ from His _____.

John 4:7 WHO did Jesus meet there?

_____

John 4:7 WHAT did Jesus ask for?

_____

John 4:10 WHAT did Jesus tell the woman He could give her?

_____

John 4:13-14 WHAT will happen to those who drink living water?

_____

_____

Did the woman believe Jesus? Did she accept the living water? ___ Yes ___ No

John 4:39-42 Did any other people believe in Jesus? ___ Yes ___ No

John 4:46 WHO did Jesus meet in Galilee?

_____

John 4:47 WHY did he come to Jesus?

_____

_____

John 4:50 WHAT did Jesus tell the royal official?

_____

John 4:50 WHAT did the royal official do?

_____

John 4:51-53 WHAT happened to the royal official's son?

_____

Did the royal official and his household believe?
___ Yes ___ No

WHAT are the two main things in John 4 (WHO are our two witnesses)?

1. the w_____ at the _____

2. the r ___ ___ ___ ___ o ___ ___ ___ ___ ___ ___ ___

Title your chapter by naming it after your two witnesses and write it on your book chart on page 137.

Well, dear friend, you are now using your very grown-up way of studying the Bible, searching out truth for yourself, "bagging and tagging it" so you can remember what you learned. There is more to learn about doing a book chart, but all that is explained in greater depth in the *New Inductive Study Bible* (NISB), which is what we suggest you save your money for or ask for as your birthday or Christmas gift, whichever comes first!

In the NISB, at the end of every book of the Bible, you'll find an "At a Glance" chart to fill out for that particular book of the Bible. When you do that, just think of what you will have! Evidence that you have studied God's Word inductively on your own so you can know truth firsthand. That's awesome, and so are you!

The Hunt for Physical Evidence

As we wrap up our last case, Molly and Max have a game for you to play with your family or friends. First you need a piece of paper for each person that's going to play this game. Then copy the list on the next page on each piece of paper. You also need a pencil and a Bible for each person to use. Get your family or friends together and give each person a list, a pencil, and a Bible.

Explain that on their list are Scripture references. Each person has to look up the Scripture reference and write down the object it names in the blank on his list. We've given you the first letter of each object. Once you have completed your list, you need to race through the house and outside to find all the objects named in the Scriptures. The first person who gathers all the objects wins the game. Let the hunt begin!

John 15:5 b __ __ __ __ __ __ __

Galatians 5:22 f __ __ __ __

Isaiah 18:5 f __ __ __ __ __

Matthew 5:13 s __ __ __

1 Corinthians 10:16 c __ __

Matthew 7:24 r __ __ __

Mark 12:42 c __ __ __

Genesis 1:30 g __ __ __ __   p __ __ __ __

John 6:35 b __ __ __ __

Matthew 24:32 l __ __ __ __ __

John at a Glance Book Chart

Chapter Themes	
1	
2	
3	
4	

Examine the Evidence

"Well, Molly, we have had a great six weeks with our inductive detectives! It's time to check out their skills."

"You're right, Max! A detective has to pass an exam in order to get a detective's license."

Are you ready, inductive detective, to take our exam and get your inductive detective's license so that you can be a full-fledged Bible detective, able to study any book in the Bible? Great! We know you'll pass with flying colors because you have done a lot of hard work and are ready to step out on your own. So let's get started. We'll be praying for you. Don't you forget to pray. In fact, before you ever take any test, you ought to ask for God's help. (Remember, though, you need to do your part and study your subject! God can't bless you when you don't do what you are supposed to do. If He did, He would be encouraging you to not study!)

Inductive Detective Exam

1. Before you begin to study the Bible, what is the first thing an inductive detective should do? ___ ___ ___ ___

2. The first step to inductive Bible study is: _____
   a. application   b. interpretation   c. observation

3. The second step to inductive Bible study is: _____
   a. application   b. interpretation   c. observation

4. The third step to inductive Bible study is : _____
   a. application   b. interpretation   c. observation

5. Match the question that goes to the correct step of Bible Study.

___ Observation

___ Interpretation

___ Application

   a. Shows how things are different

   b. What does it mean?

   c. Is a story that is true-to-life.

   d. How does the meaning of this truth apply to me?

   e. What does it say?

6. What gesture do you do to remind you of observation? _____

   a. pointing to your brain
   b. using your two hands to make circles like glasses and moving your hands away from your eyes toward your page
   c. turning your head to the right, then your body, and walking to the right

7. True or False: Context is the setting in which something is found.

8. True or False: Context is not very important in helping us to understand a Bible passage.

9. True or False: Historical context tells the time in history an event happens.

10. True or False: Cultural context shows us the customs of a group of people.

11.   When you study the Bible you look for the things that
      are obvious (easiest to see). What are the three easiest
      things to see?
      1. p _ _ _ _ e
      2. p _ _ _ _ s
      3. e _ _ _ _ s

12.   As you observe the Bible text, there are questions that
      you ask to interrogate the text, We call them the 5 W's
      and an H. List them below:
      1. _____
      2. _____
      3. _____
      4. _____
      5. _____
      6. _____

13.   _____ _____ are words that unlock the meaning
      of the chapter or book you are studying and give you
      clues about what is most important in a passage of
      Scripture.

14.   What do you do when you come across one of these
      words?_____
      a. Mark it in a special way using a special color or
         symbol to help you spot it immediately.
      b. Write it on an index card so you won't forget it.
      c. Write in the margin on your Observation Worksheet.

15.   True or False: You should not mark pronouns or
      synonyms when you mark key words.

16.   What question do you mark with a clock on your
      Observation Worksheet? w_____

17.   When you write down the facts that you observe from
      each key word, you are making a l_ _ _.

18. True or False: Contrasts show us how things are alike.

19. Write a contrast for light. _____

20. A term of _____ shows us a conclusion is being made or a result is being stated. It uses words such as *therefore, for, so that,* and *for this reason.* It tells us what it is there for.

21. What gesture do you use to remind you of interpretation?_____
    a. pointing to your brain
    b. using your two hands to make circles like glasses and moving your hands away from your eyes toward your page
    c. turning your head to the right, then your body, and walking to the right

22. When you are interpreting the Bible, there is a very important rule to remember.
    Scripture never _____ _____.

23. True or False: Context is the "boss" in interpreting Scripture.

24. True or False: In interpretation you do not look at the whole Bible. You only look at the passage you are studying.

25. True or False: In interpretation, Bible passages that are not clearly understood can be used to establish your beliefs.

26. True or False: A figure of speech is a word, a phrase, or an expression that is used in a creative, make-believe way, instead of a real way.

27. Match the definition with the correct word by putting the letter of the correct definition in the blank in front of the word.

    ____ parable

    ____ symbol

    ____ simile

    ____ metaphor

    a. an implied comparison between two things that are different
    b. a stated comparison between two different things that uses connecting words
    c. shows a contrast between two words
    d. a story that teaches a moral lesson or a truth
    e. a story that is a real story
    f. a picture or an object that stands for or represents another thing

28. True or False: Looking at a word in the language it was written will help us understand what the author meant when he used the word.

29. What are two helpful tools we use to look up words in their original language? an exhaustive c_____ and an expository d_____

30. Which verb tense is a continuing action? _____
    a. aorist   b. present   c. perfect

31. Which verb tense takes place at one point in time? _____
    a. aorist   b. present   c. perfect

32. Which verb tense has an action that has happened in the past with results that are happening in the future? _____
    a. aorist   b. present   c. perfect

33. When we compare Scripture with other Scripture it is called c_____ - r_____.

34. When we look at what time in history that Jesus was arrested, we are looking at what? _____
    a. cultural context   b. concordances   c. historical context

35. _____ charts are a way to record all the important themes that you discover as you study a book of the Bible.

36. To make a _____ chart, you need to look for the m_____ t_____ in each chapter.

37. Key words help show the _____ of a chapter or book.

38. Seeing a subject repeated shows us this. It is another word for subject and is called the _____.

39. What gesture do you do to remind you of application?
    _____
    a. pointing to your brain
    b. using your two hands to make circles like glasses and moving your hands away from your eyes toward your page
    c. turning your head to the right, then your body, and walking to the right

40. True or False: In inductive Bible study you study the Bible and discover for yourself what the Bible means.

Now let's see how you did, inductive detectives. If there were some questions you couldn't answer, you can go back over your workbook and look for the answer. But write it in a different color, so you can remember what you need to review.

When you finish you will find an answer key on page 154. Of course, you don't want to cheat and change your answers or write in answers you didn't know or find on your own, because that would be sin. It would be knowing to do good and not doing it. So don't even be tempted. Sin is never worth it.

For each answer that you got right, give yourself 5 points. Then add up all your points and write them here:_____. If you scored between 150 and 200 points, fill out the card that says "I aced the Inductive Detective's Exam in *How to Study Your Bible for Kids*" and we will send you a special coupon for a discount on a *New Inductive Study Bible* (NISB). It's just the tool you need as you study the Bible on your own!

Mission Accomplished

Wow! You did it! Double wow! Triple wow! You solved our mystery of how to study the Bible for *yourself*. Sam is so excited, we can't get him to quit jumping up and down!

"Sit, Sam! Sit!"

Look at all you've accomplished. You have learned WHAT an inductive Bible study is and the skills you need to do an inductive Bible study. These skills include how to observe the text by looking at context, searching for key words, interrogating the text by asking the 5 W's and an H questions, making lists, finding contrasts and comparisons, and looking at terms of conclusion.

You have also learned about figures of speech, how to use a concordance and different kinds of dictionaries, and how to look up cross-references. You know the importance of historical and cultural context and how to make a book chart as you study a book of the Bible. It took a lot of training and hard work, but now you're ready to study the Bible for yourself.

Don't forget all that you've learned during your training, such as: why Paul wrote the book of Titus, the importance of having sound doctrine and doing good deeds, and how to be submissive to those in authority over you. You have learned a lot about sin and how to be born again. You have seen that the only way to heaven is through Jesus, and you know how to put on the full armor of God. Isn't that exciting—being able to understand what the Bible has to say and how you are to apply it to your life?

We are so very, very proud of you! We had so much fun having you help us out at "M and M Detectives." You are now a full-fledged inductive Bible detective! If you fill out the card in the back of this book, we would like to send you a special certificate and an Inductive Detective carrying card. If you passed your Inductive Detective's Exam, make sure you fill that card out also, so we can send the special coupon to you. Then you will be able to get your very own *New Inductive Study Bible.*

Now that you know how to study the Bible, we have some fun inductive Bible studies for you to do. Each one is a different adventure. You can be an investigative reporter in *Wrong Way, Jonah,* make a movie in Part 1 *Jesus in the Spotlight,* Part 2 *Jesus—Awesome Power, Awesome Love,* and Part 3 *Jesus—To Eternity and Beyond!* Or you can help with an advice column in *Boy, Have I Got Problems!* Plus, Miss Kay and Miss Janna are working on many other studies. You keep studying. They'll keep writing!

As you leave the tree house, remember how much God loves you and wants you to have a relationship with Him. We'll be praying for you in all your new adventures.

Molly, Max, and

(Sam)

Puzzle Answers

Week One, Day One, page 12

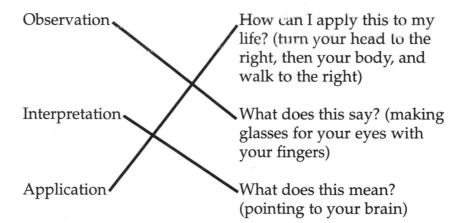

Observation ──────── How can I apply this to my life? (turn your head to the right, then your body, and walk to the right)

Interpretation ──────── What does this say? (making glasses for your eyes with your fingers)

Application ──────── What does this mean? (pointing to your brain)

Week One, Day One, page 12-13

<u>All Scripture is inspired</u>
lla cripruetS si nspideri

<u>by God and profitable for</u>
yb odG nda rotifbaelp orf

<u>teaching, for reproof,</u>
ahenicgt orf eporofr

<u>for correction, for</u>
orf oectrronic orf

<u>training in righteousness;</u>
raingnit ni ighteoussensr

<u>so that the man of God</u>
os htat het anm fo odG

<u>may</u>   <u>be</u>   <u>adequate,</u>
a y m   e b   d e q a u t e a

<u>equipped</u>   <u>for</u>   <u>every</u>
q u i p e p d e   o r f   v e r y e

<u>good</u>   <u>work</u>.
o d o g   o r k w

2 Timothy 3: <u>16</u> -<u>17</u>

Week One, Day Four, page 25

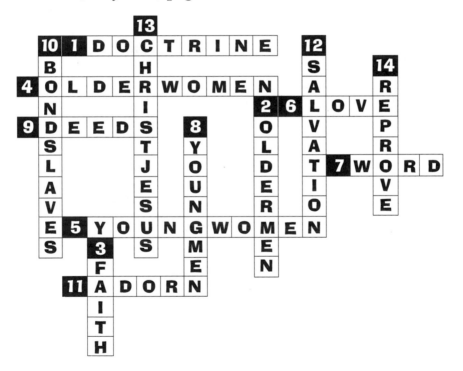

Week Two, Day Four, page 42

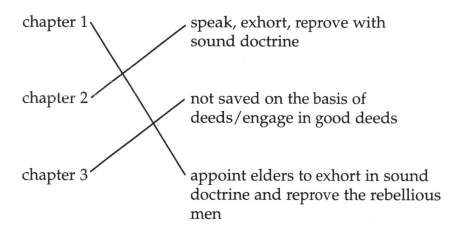

chapter 1   speak, exhort, reprove with sound doctrine

chapter 2   not saved on the basis of deeds/engage in good deeds

chapter 3   appoint elders to exhort in sound doctrine and reprove the rebellious men

Week Three, Day One, page 56

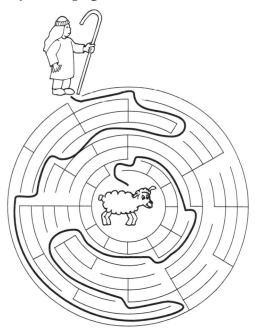

Week Three, Day Five, page 70

_d_ parable

_f_ symbol

_b_ simile

_a_ metaphor

a. an implied comparison between two things that are different

b. a stated comparison between two different things that uses connecting words

c. shows a contrast between two words

d. a story that teaches a moral lesson or a truth

e. a story that is a real story

f. a picture or an object that stands for or represents another thing

Week Four, Day One, page 76-77

B Y T H I S T H E C H I L D R E N

O F G O D A N D T H E

C H I L D R E N O F T H E D E V I L

A R E O B V I O U S: A N Y O N E

W H O D O E S N O T P R A C T I C E

RIGHTEOUSNESS IS NOT
OF GOD, NOR THE ONE
WHO DOES NOT LOVE HIS
BROTHER.

1 John 3:<u>10</u>

Week Five, Day One, page 101

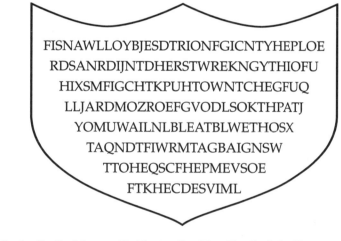

FISNAWLLOYBJESDTRIONFGICNTYHEPLOE
RDSANRDIJNTDHERSTWREKNGYTHIOFU
HIXSMFIGCHTKPUHTOWNTCHEGFUQ
LLJARDMOZROEFGVODLSOKTHPATJ
YOMUWAILNLBLEATBLWETHOSX
TAQNDTFIWRMTAGBAIGNSW
TTOHEQSCFHEPMEVSOE
FTKHECDESVIML

FINALLY, BE STRONG
IN THE LORD AND IN
THE STRENGTH OF
HIS MIGHT. PUT ON
THE FULL ARMOR
OF GOD, SO THAT
YOU WILL BE ABLE TO

<u>S T A N D</u>   <u>F I R M</u>   <u>A G A I N S T</u>
<u>T H E</u>   <u>S C H E M E S</u>   <u>O F</u>
<u>T H E</u>   <u>D E V I L</u>.

Ephesians 6: <u>10</u>-<u>11</u>

Week Five, Day Two, page 105

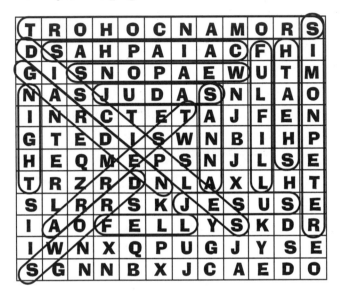

Week Five, Day Four, page 112

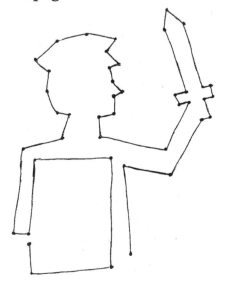

Week Six, Day Two, page 126

Here's the secret message:

YFG   GSVHV   SZEV   YVVM   DIRGGVM   HL
BUT   THESE   HAVE   BEEN   WRITTEN   SO

GSZG   BLF   NZB   YVORVEV   GSZG   QVHFH   RH
THAT   YOU   MAY   BELIEVE   THAT   JESUS   IS

GSV   XSIRHG,   GSV   HLM   LU   TLW;   ZMW
THE   CHRIST,   THE   SON   OF   GOD;   AND

GSZG   YVORVERMT   BLF   NZB   SZEV   ORUV
THAT   BELIEVING   YOU   MAY   HAVE   LIFE

RM   SRH   MZNV.
 IN   HIS   NAME.

QLSM 20:31
John 20:31

Week Six, Day Three, page 132

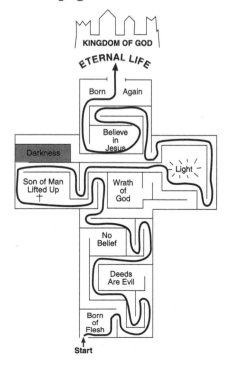

Week Six, Day Five, page 137

John at a Glance Book Chart

Chapter Themes
1 The Word Becomes Flesh
2 Wedding at Cana/Cleansing the Temple
3 Born Again
4 Woman at the Well/Royal Official

Week Six, Day Five, page 138 Inductive Detective's Exam Answer Key:
1. pray
2. c. observation
3. b. interpretation
4. a. application
5. e. Observation: What does it say?
   b. Interpretation: What does it mean?
   d. Application: How does the meaning of this truth apply to me?
6. b. using your two hands to make circles like glasses and moving your hands away from your eyes toward your page
7. True
8. False
9. True
10. True
11. people, places, events
12. Who, What, When, Where, Why, How

13. Key words
14. a. Mark it in a special way using a special color or symbol to help you spot it immediately.
15. False
16. when
17. list
18. False
19. dark
20. conclusion
21. a. pointing to your brain
22. contradicts Scripture
23. True
24. False
25. False
26. True
27. d. parable—a story that teaches a moral lesson or a truth
    f. symbol—a picture or an object that stands for or represents another thing
    b. simile—a stated comparison between two different things that uses connecting words
    a. metaphor—implied comparison between two things that are different
28. True
29. concordance, dictionary
30. b. present
31. a. aorist
32. c. perfect
33. cross-referencing
34. c. historical context
35. book
36. book, main thing
37. subject
38. theme
39. c. turning your head to the right, then your body, and walking to the right
40. True

Titus 1-3

Chapter 1

1 Paul, a bond-servant of God and an apostle of Jesus Christ, for the faith of those chosen of God and the knowledge of the truth which is according to godliness,

2 in the hope of eternal life, which God, who cannot lie, promised long ages ago,

3 but at the proper time manifested, *even* His word, in the proclamation with which I was entrusted according to the commandment of God our Savior,

4 To Titus, my true child in a common faith: Grace and peace from God the Father and Christ Jesus our Savior.

5 For this reason I left you in Crete, that you would set in order what remains and appoint elders in every city as I directed you,

6 *namely*, if any man is above reproach, the husband of one wife, having children who believe, not accused of dissipation or rebellion.

7 For the overseer must be above reproach as God's steward, not self-willed, not quick-tempered, not addicted to wine, not pugnacious, not fond of sordid gain,

8 but hospitable, loving what is good, sensible, just, devout, self-controlled,

9 holding fast the faithful word which is in accordance with the teaching, so that he will be able both to exhort in sound doctrine and to refute those who contradict.

10 For there are many rebellious men, empty talkers and deceivers, especially those of the circumcision,

11 who must be silenced because they are upsetting whole families, teaching things they should not *teach* for the sake of sordid gain.

12 One of themselves, a prophet of their own, said, "Cretans are always liars, evil beasts, lazy gluttons."

13 This testimony is true. For this reason reprove them severely so that they may be sound in the faith,

14 not paying attention to Jewish myths and commandments of men who turn away from the truth.

15 To the pure, all things are pure; but to those who are defiled and unbelieving, nothing is pure, but both their mind and their conscience are defiled.

16 They profess to know God, but by *their* deeds they deny *Him,* being detestable and disobedient and worthless for any good deed.

Chapter 2

1 But as for you, speak the things which are fitting for sound doctrine.

2 Older men are to be temperate, dignified, sensible, sound in faith, in love, in perseverance.

3 Older women likewise are to be reverent in their behavior, not malicious gossips nor enslaved to much wine, teaching what is good,

4 so that they may encourage the young women to love their husbands, to love their children,

5 *to be* sensible, pure, workers at home, kind, being subject to their own husbands, so that the word of God will not be dishonored.

6 Likewise urge the young men to be sensible;

7 in all things show yourself to be an example of good deeds, *with* purity in doctrine, dignified,

8 sound *in* speech which is beyond reproach, so that the opponent will be put to shame, having nothing bad to say about us.

9 *Urge* bondslaves to be subject to their own masters in everything, to be well-pleasing, not argumentative,

10 not pilfering, but showing all good faith so that they will adorn the doctrine of God our Savior in every respect.

11 For the grace of God has appeared, bringing salvation to all men,

12 instructing us to deny ungodliness and worldly desires and to live sensibly, righteously and godly in the present age,

13 looking for the blessed hope and the appearing of the glory of our great God and Savior, Christ Jesus,

14 who gave Himself for us to redeem us from every lawless deed, and to purify for Himself a people for His own possession, zealous for good deeds.

15 These things speak and exhort and reprove with all authority. Let no one disregard you.

Chapter 3

1 Remind them to be subject to rulers, to authorities, to be obedient, to be ready for every good deed,

2 to malign no one, to be peaceable, gentle, showing every consideration for all men.

3 For we also once were foolish ourselves, disobedient, deceived, enslaved to various lusts and pleasures, spending our life in malice and envy, hateful, hating one another.

4 But when the kindness of God our Savior and *His* love for mankind appeared,

5 He saved us, not on the basis of deeds which we have done in righteousness, but according to His mercy, by the washing of regeneration and renewing by the Holy Spirit,

6 whom He poured out upon us richly through Jesus Christ our Savior,

7 so that being justified by His grace we would be made heirs according to *the* hope of eternal life.

8 This is a trustworthy statement; and concerning these things I want you to speak confidently, so that those who have believed God will be careful to engage in good deeds. These things are good and profitable for men.

9 But avoid foolish controversies and genealogies and strife and disputes about the Law, for they are unprofitable and worthless.

10 Reject a factious man after a first and second warning,

11 knowing that such a man is perverted and is sinning, being self-condemned.

12 When I send Artemas or Tychicus to you, make every effort to come to me at Nicopolis, for I have decided to spend the winter there.

13 Diligently help Zenas the lawyer and Apollos on their way so that nothing is lacking for them.

14 Our people must also learn to engage in good deeds to meet pressing needs, so that they will not be unfruitful.

15 All who are with me greet you. Greet those who love us in *the* faith. Grace be with you all.

Luke 15

Chapter 15

1 Now all the tax collectors and the sinners were coming near Him to listen to Him.

2 Both the Pharisees and the scribes *began* to grumble, saying, "This man receives sinners and eats with them."

3 So He told them this parable, saying,

4 "What man among you, if he has a hundred sheep and has lost one of them, does not leave the ninety-nine in the open pasture and go after the one which is lost until he finds it?

5 "When he has found it, he lays it on his shoulders, rejoicing.

6 "And when he comes home, he calls together his friends and his neighbors, saying to them, 'Rejoice with me, for I have found my sheep which was lost!'

7 "I tell you that in the same way, there will be *more* joy in heaven over one sinner who repents than over ninety-nine righteous persons who need no repentance.

8 "Or what woman, if she has ten silver coins and loses one coin, does not light a lamp and sweep the house and search carefully until she finds it?

9 "When she has found it, she calls together her friends and neighbors, saying, 'Rejoice with me, for I have found the coin which I had lost!'

10 "In the same way, I tell you, there is joy in the presence of the angels of God over one sinner who repents."

11 And He said, "A man had two sons.

12 "The younger of them said to his father, 'Father, give me the share of the estate that falls to me.' So he divided his wealth between them.

13 "And not many days later, the younger son gathered everything together and went on a journey into a distant country, and there he squandered his estate with loose living.

14 "Now when he had spent everything, a severe famine occurred in that country, and he began to be impoverished.

15 "So he went and hired himself out to one of the citizens of that country, and he sent him into his fields to feed swine.

16 "And he would have gladly filled his stomach with the pods that the swine were eating, and no one was giving *anything* to him.

17 "But when he came to his senses, he said, 'How many of my father's hired men have more than enough bread, but I am dying here with hunger!

18 'I will get up and go to my father, and will say to him, "Father, I have sinned against heaven, and in your sight;

19 I am no longer worthy to be called your son; make me as one of your hired men."'

20 "So he got up and came to his father. But while he was still a long way off, his father saw him and felt compassion *for him*, and ran and embraced him and kissed him.

21 "And the son said to him, 'Father, I have sinned against heaven and in your sight; I am no longer worthy to be called your son.'

22 "But the father said to his slaves, 'Quickly bring out the best robe and put it on him, and put a ring on his hand and sandals on his feet;

23 and bring the fattened calf, kill it, and let us eat and celebrate;

24 for this son of mine was dead and has come to life again; he was lost and has been found.' And they began to celebrate.

25 "Now his older son was in the field, and when he came and approached the house, he heard music and dancing.

26 "And he summoned one of the servants and *began* inquiring what these things could be.

27 "And he said to him, 'Your brother has come, and your father has killed the fattened calf because he has received him back safe and sound.'

28 "But he became angry and was not willing to go in; and his father came out and *began* pleading with him.

29 "But he answered and said to his father, 'Look! For so many years I have been serving you and I have never neglected a command of yours; and *yet* you have never given me a young goat, so that I might celebrate with my friends;

30 but when this son of yours came, who has devoured your wealth with prostitutes, you killed the fattened calf for him.'

31 "And he said to him, 'Son, you have always been with me, and all that is mine is yours.

32 'But we had to celebrate and rejoice, for this brother of yours was dead and *has begun* to live, and *was* lost and has been found.'"

Revelation 1

Chapter 1

1 The Revelation of Jesus Christ, which God gave Him to show to His bond-servants, the things which must soon take place; and He sent and communicated *it* by His angel to His bond-servant John,

2 who testified to the word of God and to the testimony of Jesus Christ, *even* to all that he saw.

3 Blessed is he who reads and those who hear the words of the prophecy, and heed the things which are written in it; for the time is near.

4 John to the seven churches that are in Asia: Grace to you and peace, from Him who is and who was and who is to come, and from the seven Spirits who are before His throne,

5 and from Jesus Christ, the faithful witness, the firstborn of the dead, and the ruler of the kings of the earth. To Him who loves us and released us from our sins by His blood—

6 and He has made us *to be* a kingdom, priests to His God and Father— to Him *be* the glory and the dominion forever and ever. Amen.

7 BEHOLD, HE IS COMING WITH THE CLOUDS, and every eye will see Him, even those who pierced Him; and all the tribes of the earth will mourn over Him. So it is to be. Amen.

8 "I am the Alpha and the Omega," says the Lord God, "who is and who was and who is to come, the Almighty."

9 I, John, your brother and fellow partaker in the tribulation and kingdom and perseverance *which are* in Jesus, was on the island called Patmos because of the word of God and the testimony of Jesus.

10 I was in the Spirit on the Lord's day, and I heard behind me a loud voice like *the sound* of a trumpet,

11 saying, "Write in a book what you see, and send *it* to the seven churches: to Ephesus and to Smyrna and to Pergamum and to Thyatira and to Sardis and to Philadelphia and to Laodicea."

12 Then I turned to see the voice that was speaking with me. And having turned I saw seven golden lampstands;

13 and in the middle of the lampstands *I saw* one like a son of man, clothed in a robe reaching to the feet, and girded across His chest with a golden sash.

14 His head and His hair were white like white wool, like snow; and His eyes were like a flame of fire.

15 His feet *were* like burnished bronze, when it has been made to glow in a furnace, and His voice *was* like the sound of many waters.

16 In His right hand He held seven stars, and out of His mouth came a sharp two-edged sword; and His face was like the sun shining in its strength.

17 When I saw Him, I fell at His feet like a dead man. And He placed His right hand on me, saying, "Do not be afraid; I am the first and the last,

18 and the living One; and I was dead, and behold, I am alive forevermore, and I have the keys of death and of Hades.

19 "Therefore write the things which you have seen, and the things which are, and the things which will take place after these things.

20 "As for the mystery of the seven stars which you saw in My right hand, and the seven golden lampstands: the seven stars are the angels of the seven churches, and the seven lampstands are the seven churches."

1 John 2,3

Chapter 2

1 My little children, I am writing these things to you so that you may not sin. And if anyone sins, we have an Advocate with the Father, Jesus Christ the righteous;

2 and He Himself is the propitiation for our sins; and not for ours only, but also for *those of* the whole world.

3 By this we know that we have come to know Him, if we keep His commandments.

4 The one who says, "I have come to know Him," and does not keep His commandments, is a liar, and the truth is not in him;

5 but whoever keeps His word, in him the love of God has truly been perfected. By this we know that we are in Him:

6 the one who says he abides in Him ought himself to walk in the same manner as He walked.

7 Beloved, I am not writing a new commandment to you, but an old commandment which you have had from the beginning; the old commandment is the word which you have heard.

8 On the other hand, I am writing a new commandment to you, which is true in Him and in you, because the darkness is passing away and the true Light is already shining.

9 The one who says he is in the Light and *yet* hates his brother is in the darkness until now.

10 The one who loves his brother abides in the Light and there is no cause for stumbling in him.

11 But the one who hates his brother is in the darkness and walks in the darkness, and does not know where he is going because the darkness has blinded his eyes.

12 I am writing to you, little children, because your sins have been forgiven you for His name's sake.

13 I am writing to you, fathers, because you know Him who has been from the beginning. I am writing to you, young men, because you have overcome the evil one. I have written to you, children, because you know the Father.

14 I have written to you, fathers, because you know Him who has been from the beginning. I have written to you, young men, because you are strong, and the word of God abides in you, and you have overcome the evil one.

15 Do not love the world nor the things in the world. If anyone loves the world, the love of the Father is not in him.

16 For all that is in the world, the lust of the flesh and the lust of the eyes and the boastful pride of life, is not from the Father, but is from the world.

17 The world is passing away, and *also* its lusts; but the one who does the will of God lives forever.

18 Children, it is the last hour; and just as you heard that antichrist is coming, even now many antichrists have appeared; from this we know that it is the last hour.

19 They went out from us, but they were not *really* of us; for if they had been of us, they would have remained with us; but *they went out,* so that it would be shown that they all are not of us.

20 But you have an anointing from the Holy One, and you all know.

21 I have not written to you because you do not know the truth, but because you do know it, and because no lie is of the truth.

22 Who is the liar but the one who denies that Jesus is the Christ? This is the antichrist, the one who denies the Father and the Son.

23 Whoever denies the Son does not have the Father; the one who confesses the Son has the Father also.

24 As for you, let that abide in you which you heard from the beginning. If what you heard from the beginning abides in you, you also will abide in the Son and in the Father.

25 This is the promise which He Himself made to us: eternal life.

26 These things I have written to you concerning those who are trying to deceive you.

27 As for you, the anointing which you received from Him abides in you, and you have no need for anyone to teach you; but as His anointing teaches you about all things, and is true and is not a lie, and just as it has taught you, you abide in Him.

28 Now, little children, abide in Him, so that when He appears, we may have confidence and not shrink away from Him in shame at His coming.

29 If you know that He is righteous, you know that everyone also who practices righteousness is born of Him.

Chapter 3

1 See how great a love the Father has bestowed on us, that we would be called children of God; and *such* we are. For this reason the world does not know us, because it did not know Him.

2 Beloved, now we are children of God, and it has not appeared as yet what we will be. We know that when He appears, we will be like Him, because we will see Him just as He is.

3 And everyone who has this hope *fixed* on Him purifies himself, just as He is pure.

4 Everyone who practices sin also practices lawlessness; and sin is lawlessness.

5 You know that He appeared in order to take away sins; and in Him there is no sin.

6 No one who abides in Him sins; no one who sins has seen Him or knows Him.

7 Little children, make sure no one deceives you; the one who practices righteousness is righteous, just as He is righteous;

8 the one who practices sin is of the devil; for the devil has sinned from the beginning. The Son of God appeared for this purpose, to destroy the works of the devil.

9 No one who is born of God practices sin, because His seed abides in him; and he cannot sin, because he is born of God.

10 By this the children of God and the children of the devil are obvious: anyone who does not practice righteousness is not of God, nor the one who does not love his brother.

11 For this is the message which you have heard from the beginning, that we should love one another;

12 not as Cain, *who* was of the evil one and slew his brother. And for what reason did he slay him? Because his deeds were evil, and his brother's were righteous.

13 Do not be surprised, brethren, if the world hates you.

14 We know that we have passed out of death into life, because we love the brethren. He who does not love abides in death.

15 Everyone who hates his brother is a murderer; and you know that no murderer has eternal life abiding in him.

16 We know love by this, that He laid down His life for us; and we ought to lay down our lives for the brethren.

17 But whoever has the world's goods, and sees his brother in need and closes his heart against him, how does the love of God abide in him?

18 Little children, let us not love with word or with tongue, but in deed and truth.

19 We will know by this that we are of the truth, and will assure our heart before Him

20 in whatever our heart condemns us; for God is greater than our heart and knows all things.

21 Beloved, if our heart does not condemn us, we have confidence before God;

22 and whatever we ask we receive from Him, because we keep His commandments and do the things that are pleasing in His sight.

23 This is His commandment, that we believe in the name of His Son Jesus Christ, and love one another, just as He commanded us.

24 The one who keeps His commandments abides in Him, and He in him. We know by this that He abides in us, by the Spirit whom He has given us.

Ephesians 6

Chapter 6

1 Children, obey your parents in the Lord, for this is right.

2 HONOR YOUR FATHER AND MOTHER (which is the first commandment with a promise),

3 SO THAT IT MAY BE WELL WITH YOU, AND THAT YOU MAY LIVE LONG ON THE EARTH.

4 Fathers, do not provoke your children to anger, but bring them up in the discipline and instruction of the Lord.

5 Slaves, be obedient to those who are your masters according to the flesh, with fear and trembling, in the sincerity of your heart, as to Christ;

6 not by way of eyeservice, as men-pleasers, but as slaves of Christ, doing the will of God from the heart.

7 With good will render service, as to the Lord, and not to men,

8 knowing that whatever good thing each one does, this he will receive back from the Lord, whether slave or free.

9 And masters, do the same things to them, and give up threatening, knowing that both their Master and yours is in heaven, and there is no partiality with Him.

10 Finally, be strong in the Lord and in the strength of His might.

11 Put on the full armor of God, so that you will be able to stand firm against the schemes of the devil.

12 For our struggle is not against flesh and blood, but against the rulers, against the powers, against the world forces of this darkness, against the spiritual *forces* of wickedness in the heavenly *places*.

13 Therefore, take up the full armor of God, so that you will be able to resist in the evil day, and having done everything, to stand firm.

14 Stand firm therefore, HAVING GIRDED YOUR LOINS WITH TRUTH, and HAVING PUT ON THE BREASTPLATE OF RIGHTEOUSNESS,

15 and having shod YOUR FEET WITH THE PREPARATION OF THE GOSPEL OF PEACE;

16 in addition to all, taking up the shield of faith with which you will be able to extinguish all the flaming arrows of the evil *one*.

17 And take THE HELMET OF SALVATION, and the sword of the Spirit, which is the word of God.

18 With all prayer and petition pray at all times in the Spirit, and with this in view, be on the alert with all perseverance and petition for all the saints,

19 and *pray* on my behalf, that utterance may be given to me in the opening of my mouth, to make known with boldness the mystery of the gospel,

20 for which I am an ambassador in chains; that in *proclaiming* it I may speak boldly, as I ought to speak.

21 But that you also may know about my circumstances, how I am doing, Tychicus, the beloved brother and faithful minister in the Lord, will make everything known to you.

22 I have sent him to you for this very purpose, so that you may know about us, and that he may comfort your hearts.

23 Peace be to the brethren, and love with faith, from God the Father and the Lord Jesus Christ.

24 Grace be with all those who love our Lord Jesus Christ with incorruptible *love*.

John 1–4

Chapter 1

1 In the beginning was the Word, and the Word was with God, and the Word was God.

2 He was in the beginning with God.

3 All things came into being through Him, and apart from Him nothing came into being that has come into being.

4 In Him was life, and the life was the Light of men.

5 The Light shines in the darkness, and the darkness did not comprehend it.

6 There came a man sent from God, whose name was John.

7 He came as a witness, to testify about the Light, so that all might believe through him.

8 He was not the Light, but *he came* to testify about the Light.

9 There was the true Light which, coming into the world, enlightens every man.

10 He was in the world, and the world was made through Him, and the world did not know Him.

11 He came to His own, and those who were His own did not receive Him.

12 But as many as received Him, to them He gave the right to become children of God, *even* to those who believe in His name,

13 who were born, not of blood nor of the will of the flesh nor of the will of man, but of God.

14 And the Word became flesh, and dwelt among us, and we saw His glory, glory as of the only begotten from the Father, full of grace and truth.

15 John testified about Him and cried out, saying, "This was He of whom I said, 'He who comes after me has a higher rank than I, for He existed before me.'"

16 For of His fullness we have all received, and grace upon grace.

17 For the Law was given through Moses; grace and truth were realized through Jesus Christ.

18 No one has seen God at any time; the only begotten God who is in the bosom of the Father, He has explained *Him.*

19 This is the testimony of John, when the Jews sent to him priests and Levites from Jerusalem to ask him, "Who are you?"

20 And he confessed and did not deny, but confessed, "I am not the Christ."

21 They asked him, "What then? Are you Elijah?" And he said, "I am not." "Are you the Prophet?" And he answered, "No."

22 Then they said to him, "Who are you, so that we may give an answer to those who sent us? What do you say about yourself?"

23 He said, "I am A VOICE OF ONE CRYING IN THE WILDERNESS, 'MAKE STRAIGHT THE WAY OF THE LORD,' as Isaiah the prophet said."

24 Now they had been sent from the Pharisees.

25 They asked him, and said to him, "Why then are you baptizing, if you are not the Christ, nor Elijah, nor the Prophet?"

26 John answered them saying, "I baptize in water, *but* among you stands One whom you do not know.

27 "*It is* He who comes after me, the thong of whose sandal I am not worthy to untie."

28 These things took place in Bethany beyond the Jordan, where John was baptizing.

29 The next day he saw Jesus coming to him and said, "Behold, the Lamb of God who takes away the sin of the world!

30 "This is He on behalf of whom I said, 'After me comes a Man who has a higher rank than I, for He existed before me.'

31 "I did not recognize Him, but so that He might be manifested to Israel, I came baptizing in water."

32 John testified saying, "I have seen the Spirit descending as a dove out of heaven, and He remained upon Him.

33 "I did not recognize Him, but He who sent me to baptize in water said to me, 'He upon whom you see the Spirit descending and remaining upon Him, this is the One who baptizes in the Holy Spirit.'

34 "I myself have seen, and have testified that this is the Son of God."

35 Again the next day John was standing with two of his disciples,

36 and he looked at Jesus as He walked, and said, "Behold, the Lamb of God!"

37 The two disciples heard him speak, and they followed Jesus.

38 And Jesus turned and saw them following, and said to them, "What do you seek?" They said to Him, "Rabbi (which translated means Teacher), where are You staying?"

39 He said to them, "Come, and you will see." So they came and saw where He was staying; and they stayed with Him that day, for it was about the tenth hour.

40 One of the two who heard John *speak* and followed Him, was Andrew, Simon Peter's brother.

41 He found first his own brother Simon and said to him, "We have found the Messiah" (which translated means Christ).

42 He brought him to Jesus. Jesus looked at him and said, "You are Simon the son of John; you shall be called Cephas" (which is translated Peter).

43 The next day He purposed to go into Galilee, and He found Philip. And Jesus said to him, "Follow Me."

44 Now Philip was from Bethsaida, of the city of Andrew and Peter.

45 Philip found Nathanael and said to him, "We have found Him of whom Moses in the Law and *also* the Prophets wrote—Jesus of Nazareth, the son of Joseph."

46 Nathanael said to him, "Can any good thing come out of Nazareth?" Philip said to him, "Come and see."

47 Jesus saw Nathanael coming to Him, and said of him, "Behold, an Israelite indeed, in whom there is no deceit!"

48 Nathanael said to Him, "How do You know me?" Jesus answered and said to him, "Before Philip called you, when you were under the fig tree, I saw you."

49 Nathanael answered Him, "Rabbi, You are the Son of God; You are the King of Israel."

50 Jesus answered and said to him, "Because I said to you that I saw you under the fig tree, do you believe? You will see greater things than these."

51 And He said to him, "Truly, truly, I say to you, you will see the heavens opened and the angels of God ascending and descending on the Son of Man."

Chapter 2

1 On the third day there was a wedding in Cana of Galilee, and the mother of Jesus was there;

2 and both Jesus and His disciples were invited to the wedding.

3 When the wine ran out, the mother of Jesus said to Him, "They have no wine."

4 And Jesus said to her, "Woman, what does that have to do with us? My hour has not yet come."

5 His mother said to the servants, "Whatever He says to you, do it."

6 Now there were six stone waterpots set there for the Jewish custom of purification, containing twenty or thirty gallons each.

7 Jesus said to them, "Fill the waterpots with water." So they filled them up to the brim.

8 And He said to them, "Draw *some* out now and take it to the headwaiter." So they took it *to him.*

9 When the headwaiter tasted the water which had become wine, and did not know where it came from (but the servants who had drawn the water knew), the headwaiter called the bridegroom,

10 and said to him, "Every man serves the good wine first, and when *the people* have drunk freely, *then he serves* the poorer *wine; but* you have kept the good wine until now."

11 This beginning of *His* signs Jesus did in Cana of Galilee, and manifested His glory, and His disciples believed in Him.

12 After this He went down to Capernaum, He and His mother and *His* brothers and His disciples; and they stayed there a few days.

13 The Passover of the Jews was near, and Jesus went up to Jerusalem.

14 And He found in the temple those who were selling oxen and sheep and doves, and the money changers seated *at their tables.*

15 And He made a scourge of cords, and drove *them* all out of the temple, with the sheep and the oxen; and He poured out the coins of the money changers and overturned their tables;

16 and to those who were selling the doves He said, "Take these things away; stop making My Father's house a place of business."

17 His disciples remembered that it was written, "ZEAL FOR YOUR HOUSE WILL CONSUME ME."

18 The Jews then said to Him, "What sign do You show us as your authority for doing these things?"

19 Jesus answered them, "Destroy this temple, and in three days I will raise it up."

20 The Jews then said, "It took forty-six years to build this temple, and will You raise it up in three days?"

21 But He was speaking of the temple of His body.

22 So when He was raised from the dead, His disciples remembered that He said this; and they believed the Scripture and the word which Jesus had spoken.

23 Now when He was in Jerusalem at the Passover, during the feast, many believed in His name, observing His signs which He was doing.

24 But Jesus, on His part, was not entrusting Himself to them, for He knew all men,

25 and because He did not need anyone to testify concerning man, for He Himself knew what was in man.

Chapter 3

1 Now there was a man of the Pharisees, named Nicodemus, a ruler of the Jews;

2 this man came to Jesus by night and said to Him, "Rabbi, we know that You have come from God *as* a teacher; for no one can do these signs that You do unless God is with him."

3 Jesus answered and said to him, "Truly, truly, I say to you, unless one is born again he cannot see the kingdom of God."

4 Nicodemus said to Him, "How can a man be born when he is old? He cannot enter a second time into his mother's womb and be born, can he?"

5 Jesus answered, "Truly, truly, I say to you, unless one is born of water and the Spirit he cannot enter into the kingdom of God.

6 "That which is born of the flesh is flesh, and that which is born of the Spirit is spirit.

7 "Do not be amazed that I said to you, 'You must be born again.'

8 "The wind blows where it wishes and you hear the sound of it, but do not know where it comes from and where it is going; so is everyone who is born of the Spirit."

9 Nicodemus said to Him, "How can these things be?"

10 Jesus answered and said to him, "Are you the teacher of Israel and do not understand these things?

11 "Truly, truly, I say to you, we speak of what we know and testify of what we have seen, and you do not accept our testimony.

12 "If I told you earthly things and you do not believe, how will you believe if I tell you heavenly things?

13 "No one has ascended into heaven, but He who descended from heaven: the Son of Man.

14 "As Moses lifted up the serpent in the wilderness, even so must the Son of Man be lifted up;

15 so that whoever believes will in Him have eternal life.

16 "For God so loved the world, that He gave His only begotten Son, that whoever believes in Him shall not perish, but have eternal life.

17 "For God did not send the Son into the world to judge the world, but that the world might be saved through Him.

18 "He who believes in Him is not judged; he who does not believe has been judged already, because he has not believed in the name of the only begotten Son of God.

19 "This is the judgment, that the Light has come into the world, and men loved the darkness rather than the Light, for their deeds were evil.

20 "For everyone who does evil hates the Light, and does not come to the Light for fear that his deeds will be exposed.

21 "But he who practices the truth comes to the Light, so that his deeds may be manifested as having been wrought in God."

22 After these things Jesus and His disciples came into the land of Judea, and there He was spending time with them and baptizing.

23 John also was baptizing in Aenon near Salim, because there was much water there; and *people* were coming and were being baptized—

24 for John had not yet been thrown into prison.

25   Therefore there arose a discussion on the part of John's disciples with a Jew about purification.

26   And they came to John and said to him, "Rabbi, He who was with you beyond the Jordan, to whom you have testified, behold, He is baptizing and all are coming to Him."

27   John answered and said, "A man can receive nothing unless it has been given him from heaven.

28   "You yourselves are my witnesses that I said, 'I am not the Christ,' but, 'I have been sent ahead of Him.'

29   "He who has the bride is the bridegroom; but the friend of the bridegroom, who stands and hears him, rejoices greatly because of the bridegroom's voice. So this joy of mine has been made full.

30   "He must increase, but I must decrease.

31   "He who comes from above is above all, he who is of the earth is from the earth and speaks of the earth. He who comes from heaven is above all.

32   "What He has seen and heard, of that He testifies; and no one receives His testimony.

33   "He who has received His testimony has set his seal to *this*, that God is true.

34   "For He whom God has sent speaks the words of God; for He gives the Spirit without measure.

35   "The Father loves the Son and has given all things into His hand.

36   "He who believes in the Son has eternal life; but he who does not obey the Son will not see life, but the wrath of God abides on him."

Chapter 4

1   Therefore when the Lord knew that the Pharisees had heard that Jesus was making and baptizing more disciples than John

2   (although Jesus Himself was not baptizing, but His disciples were),

3   He left Judea and went away again into Galilee.

4   And He had to pass through ᵃSamaria.

5   So He came to a city of Samaria called Sychar, near the parcel of ground that Jacob gave to his son Joseph;

6   and Jacob's well was there. So Jesus, being wearied from His journey, was sitting thus by the well. It was about the sixth hour.

7   There came a woman of Samaria to draw water. Jesus said to her, "Give Me a drink."

8   For His disciples had gone away into the city to buy food.

9   Therefore the Samaritan woman said to Him, "How is it that You, being a Jew, ask me for a drink since I am a Samaritan woman?" (For Jews have no dealings with Samaritans.)

10   Jesus answered and said to her, "If you knew the gift of God, and who it is who says to you, 'Give Me a drink,' you would have asked Him, and He would have given you living water."

11   She said to Him, "Sir, You have nothing to draw with and the well is deep; where then do You get that living water?

12   "You are not greater than our father Jacob, are You, who gave us the well, and drank of it himself and his sons and his cattle?"

13   Jesus answered and said to her, "Everyone who drinks of this water will thirst again;

14   but whoever drinks of the water that I will give him shall never thirst; but the water that I will give him will become in him a well of water springing up to eternal life."

15   The woman said to Him, "Sir, give me this water, so I will not be thirsty nor come all the way here to draw."

16   He said to her, "Go, call your husband and come here."

17   The woman answered and said, "I have no husband." Jesus said to her, "You have correctly said, 'I have no husband';

18 for you have had five husbands, and the one whom you now have is not your husband; this you have said truly."

19 The woman said to Him, "Sir, I perceive that You are a prophet.

20 "Our fathers worshiped in this mountain, and you *people* say that in Jerusalem is the place where men ought to worship."

21 Jesus said to her, "Woman, believe Me, an hour is coming when neither in this mountain nor in Jerusalem will you worship the Father.

22 "You worship what you do not know; we worship what we know, for salvation is from the Jews.

23 "But an hour is coming, and now is, when the true worshipers will worship the Father in spirit and truth; for such people the Father seeks to be His worshipers.

24 "God is spirit, and those who worship Him must worship in spirit and truth."

25 The woman said to Him, "I know that Messiah is coming (He who is called Christ); when that One comes, He will declare all things to us."

26 Jesus said to her, "I who speak to you am *He.*"

27 At this point His disciples came, and they were amazed that He had been speaking with a woman, yet no one said, "What do You seek?" or, "Why do You speak with her?"

28 So the woman left her waterpot, and went into the city and said to the men,

29 "Come, see a man who told me all the things that I *have* done; this is not the Christ, is it?"

30 They went out of the city, and were coming to Him.

31 Meanwhile the disciples were urging Him, saying, "Rabbi, eat."

32 But He said to them, "I have food to eat that you do not know about."

33 So the disciples were saying to one another, "No one brought Him *anything* to eat, did he?"

34 Jesus said to them, "My food is to do the will of Him who sent Me and to accomplish His work.

35 "Do you not say, 'There are yet four months, and *then* comes the harvest'? Behold, I say to you, lift up your eyes and look on the fields, that they are white for harvest.

36 "Already he who reaps is receiving wages and is gathering fruit for life eternal; so that he who sows and he who reaps may rejoice together.

37 "For in this *case* the saying is true, 'One sows and another reaps.'

38 "I sent you to reap that for which you have not labored; others have labored and you have entered into their labor."

39 From that city many of the Samaritans believed in Him because of the word of the woman who testified, "He told me all the things that I *have* done."

40 So when the Samaritans came to Jesus, they were asking Him to stay with them; and He stayed there two days.

41 Many more believed because of His word;

42 and they were saying to the woman, "It is no longer because of what you said that we believe, for we have heard for ourselves and know that this One is indeed the Savior of the world."

43 After the two days He went forth from there into Galilee.

44 For Jesus Himself testified that a prophet has no honor in his own country.

45 So when He came to Galilee, the Galileans received Him, having seen all the things that He did in Jerusalem at the feast; for they themselves also went to the feast.

46 Therefore He came again to Cana of Galilee where He had made the water wine. And there was a royal official whose son was sick at Capernaum.

47 When he heard that Jesus had come out of Judea into Galilee, he went to Him and was imploring *Him* to come down and heal his son; for he was at the point of death.

48 So Jesus said to him, "Unless you *people* see signs and wonders, you *simply* will not believe."

49 The royal official said to Him, "Sir, come down before my child dies."

50 Jesus said to him, "Go; your son lives." The man believed the word that Jesus spoke to him and started off.

51 As he was now going down, *his* slaves met him, saying that his son was living.

52 So he inquired of them the hour when he began to get better. Then they said to him, "Yesterday at the seventh hour the fever left him."

53 So the father knew that *it was* at that hour in which Jesus said to him, "Your son lives"; and he himself believed and his whole household.

54 This is again a second sign that Jesus performed when He had come out of Judea into Galilee.

John 18

Chapter 18

1 When Jesus had spoken these words, He went forth with His disciples over the ravine of the Kidron, where there was a garden, in which He entered with His disciples.

2 Now Judas also, who was betraying Him, knew the place, for Jesus had often met there with His disciples.

3 Judas then, having received the *Roman* cohort and officers from the chief priests and the Pharisees, came there with lanterns and torches and weapons.

4 So Jesus, knowing all the things that were coming upon Him, went forth and said to them, "Whom do you seek?"

5 They answered Him, "Jesus the Nazarene." He said to them, "I am *He.*" And Judas also, who was betraying Him, was standing with them.

6 So when He said to them, "I am *He,*" they drew back and fell to the ground.

7 Therefore He again asked them, "Whom do you seek?" And they said, "Jesus the Nazarene."

8 Jesus answered, "I told you that I am *He;* so if you seek Me, let these go their way,"

9 to fulfill the word which He spoke, "Of those whom You have given Me I lost not one."

10 Simon Peter then, having a sword, drew it and struck the high priest's slave, and cut off his right ear; and the slave's name was Malchus.

11 So Jesus said to Peter, "Put the sword into the sheath; the cup which the Father has given Me, shall I not drink it?"

12 So the *Roman* cohort and the commander and the officers of the Jews, arrested Jesus and bound Him,

13 and led Him to Annas first; for he was father-in-law of Caiaphas, who was high priest that year.

14 Now Caiaphas was the one who had advised the Jews that it was expedient for one man to die on behalf of the people.

15 Simon Peter was following Jesus, and *so was* another disciple. Now that disciple was known to the high priest, and entered with Jesus into *b*the court of the high priest,

16 but Peter was standing at the door outside. So the other disciple, who was known to the high priest, went out and spoke to the doorkeeper, and brought Peter in.

17 Then the slave-girl who kept the door said to Peter, "You are not also *one* of this man's disciples, are you?" He said, "I am not."

18 Now the slaves and the officers were standing *there*, having made a charcoal fire, for it was cold and they were warming themselves; and Peter was also with them, standing and warming himself.

19 The high priest then questioned Jesus about His disciples, and about His teaching.

20 Jesus answered him, "I have spoken openly to the world; I always taught in synagogues and in the temple, where all the Jews come together; and I spoke nothing in secret.

21 "Why do you question Me? Question those who have heard what I spoke to them; they know what I said."

22 When He had said this, one of the officers standing nearby struck Jesus, saying, "Is that the way You answer the high priest?"

23 Jesus answered him, "If I have spoken wrongly, testify of the wrong; but if rightly, why do you strike Me?"

24 So Annas sent Him bound to Caiaphas the high priest.

25 Now Simon Peter was standing and warming himself. So they said to him, "You are not also *one* of His disciples, are you?" He denied *it*, and said, "I am not."

26 One of the slaves of the high priest, being a relative of the one whose ear Peter cut off, said, "Did I not see you in the garden with Him?"

27 Peter then denied *it* again, and immediately a rooster crowed.

28 Then they led Jesus from Caiaphas into the Praetorium, and it was early; and they themselves did not enter into the Praetorium so that they would not be defiled, but might eat the Passover.

29 Therefore Pilate went out to them and said, "What accusation do you bring against this Man?"

30 They answered and said to him, "If this Man were not an evildoer, we would not have delivered Him to you."

31 So Pilate said to them, "Take Him yourselves, and judge Him according to your law." The Jews said to him, "We are not permitted to put anyone to death,"

32 to fulfill the word of Jesus which He spoke, signifying by what kind of death He was about to die.

33 Therefore Pilate entered again into the Praetorium, and summoned Jesus and said to Him, "Are You the King of the Jews?"

34 Jesus answered, "Are you saying this on your own initiative, or did others tell you about Me?"

35 Pilate answered, "I am not a Jew, am I? Your own nation and the chief priests delivered You to me; what have You done?"

36 Jesus answered, "*a*My kingdom is not of this world. If My kingdom were of this world, then My servants would be fighting so that I would not be handed over to the Jews; but as it is, My kingdom is not of this realm."

37 Therefore Pilate said to Him, "So You are a king?" Jesus answered, "You say *correctly* that I am a king. For this I have been born, and for this I have come into the world, to testify to the truth. Everyone who is of the truth hears My voice."

38 Pilate said to Him, "What is truth?" And when he had said this, he went out again to the Jews and said to them, "I find no guilt in Him.

39 "But you have a custom that I release someone for you at the Passover; do you wish then that I release for you the King of the Jews?"

40 So they cried out again, saying, "Not this Man, but Barabbas." Now Barabbas was a robber.

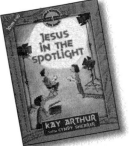

Kay Arthur and Cyndy Shearer
Kids "make" a movie to discover who Jesus is and His impact on their lives. Activities and 15-minute lessons make this study of John 1–10 great for all ages!

ISBN 0-7369-0119-1

Kay Arthur, Janna Arndt, Lisa Guest, and Cyndy Shearer
This book picks up where *Jesus in the Spotlight* leaves off: John 11–16. Kids join a movie team to bring the life of Jesus to the big screen in order to learn key truths about prayer, heaven, and Jesus.

ISBN 0-7369-0144-2

Kay Arthur and Janna Arndt
As "advice columnists," kids delve into the book of James to discover—and learn how to apply—the best answers for a variety of problems.

ISBN 0-7369-0148-5

Kay Arthur and Janna Arndt
This easy-to-use Bible study combines serious commitment to God's Word with illustrations and activities that reinforce biblical truth.

ISBN 0-7369-0362-3

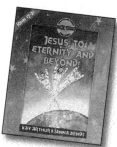

Kay Arthur and Janna Arndt
Focusing on John 17–21, children become "directors" who must discover the details of Jesus' life to make a great movie. They also learn how to get the most out of reading their Bibles.

ISBN 0-7369-0546-4

Kay Arthur and Scoti Domeij
As "reporters," kids investigate Jonah's story and conduct interviews. Using puzzles and activities, these lessons highlight God's loving care and the importance of obedience.

ISBN 0-7369-0203-1

Kay Arthur and Janna Arndt
Kids become archaeologists to uncover how God deals with sin, where different languages and nations came from, and what God's plan is for saving people (Genesis 3–11).

ISBN 0-7369-0374-7

Kay Arthur and Janna Arndt
God's Amazing Creation covers Genesis 1–2—those awesome days when God created the stars, the world, the sea, the animals, and the very first people. Young explorers will go on an archaeological dig to discover truths for themselves!

ISBN 0-7369-0143-4

Kay Arthur and Janna Arndt
The Lord's Prayer is the foundation of this special basic training, and it's not long before the trainees discover the awesome truth that God wants to talk to them as much as they want to talk to Him!

ISBN 0-7369-0666-5

Kay Arthur and Janna Arndt
Readers head out on the rugged Oregon Trail to discover the lessons Abraham learned when he left his home and moved to an unknown land. Kids will face the excitement, fears, and blessings of faith.

ISBN 0-7369-0936-2

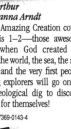

Kay Arthur and Janna Arndt
This exciting new book leads the reader on a journey to God's heart using the inductive study method and the wonder of an adventurous spy tale.

ISBN 0-7369-1161-8

Everybody, Everywhere, Anytime, Anyplace, Any Age...
Can Discover the Truth for Themselves

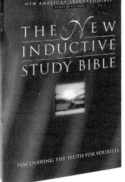

In today's world with its often confusing and mixed messages, where can you turn to find the answer to the challenges you and your family face? Whose word can you trust? Where can you turn when you need answers—about relationships, your children, your future?

The <u>Updated</u> New Inductive Study Bible

Open *this* study Bible and you will soon discover its uniqueness— unlike any other, this study Bible offers no notes, commentaries, or the opinions of others telling you what the Scripture is saying. It is in fact the only study Bible based entirely on the *inductive* study approach, providing you with instructions and the tools for observing what the text really says, interpreting what it means, and applying its principles to your life.

The only study Bible containing the *inductive study method* taught and endorsed by Kay Arthur and Precept Ministries.

• A new *smaller* size makes it easier to carry • individualized instructions for studying *every* book • guides for color marking keywords and themes • *Updated* NASB text • *improved* in-text maps and charts • 24 pages of full-color charts, historical timelines, & maps • self-discovery in its truest form

One Message, The Bible.

A SIMPLE, PROVEN APPROACH TO LETTING GOD'S WORD CHANGE YOUR LIFE...FOREVER

One Method, Inductive.

Experience the inductive study method—for a free excerpt call:
1-800-763-8280
or visit www.inductivestudy.com

Available at bookstores everywhere
HARVEST HOUSE PUBLISHERS
Eugene, Oregon 97402

BOOKS IN THE
NEW INDUCTIVE STUDY SERIES

Teach Me Your Ways
Genesis, Exodus,
Leviticus, Numbers,
Deuteronomy

Choosing Victory,
Overcoming Defeat
Joshua, Judges, Ruth

Desiring God's Own Heart
1 & 2 Samuel,
1 Chronicles

Come Walk in My Ways
1 & 2 Kings, 2 Chronicles

Overcoming Fear
and Discouragement
Ezra, Nehemiah, Esther

Trusting God
in Times of Adversity
Job

God's Blueprint for
Bible Prophecy
Daniel

Opening the Windows
of Blessings
Haggai, Zechariah,
Malachi

The Call to Follow Jesus
Luke

The Holy Spirit
Unleashed in You
Acts

God's Answers for
Relationships and Passions
1 & 2 Corinthians

Free from Bondage
God's Way
Galatians, Ephesians

That I May Know Him
Philippians, Colossians

Standing Firm in
These Last Days
1 & 2 Thessalonians

Walking in Power,
Love, and Discipline
1 & 2 Timothy, Titus

Living with Discernment
in the End Times
1 & 2 Peter, Jude

Behold, Jesus Is Coming!
Revelation

I I'd Rather Have Jesus

I'd rather have Jesus than silver or gold;
I'd rather be His than have riches untold;
I'd rather have Jesus than ~~houses and~~ houses or lands.
I'd rather be led by His nailpierced hand

ref:
   than to be the king of a vast domain
   And be held in sin's dread sway.
   I'd rather have Jesus than anything
   This world affords today.

II I'd rather have Jesus than men's applause;
   I'd rather be faithful to His dear cause;
   I'd rather have Jesus than worldwide fame.
   I'd rather be true to His holy name

III
   ~~I'd rather~~
   He's fairer than lilies of rarest bloom;
   He's sweeter than honey from out the comb;
   He's all that my hungering spirit needs.
   I'd rather have Jesus and let Him lead

Heaven came down

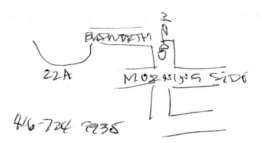

BLANDESM

22A

MORNING SIDE

416-724-9235

Arnel Alfaro

7 Bank of Montreal

Barbob Vanrob

416 - 438 - 4286 - Spherin Diana Runne

www. spherin. ca

His Eye Is on the Sparrow

I

Why should I feel discouraged?
Why should the shadows come?
Why should my heart be lonely
And long for heav'n and home
When Jesus is my portion?
My constant Friend is He:

Chorus:

His eye is on the sparrow,
And I know He watches me.
His eye is on the sparrow
And I know He watches me.

Refrain

I sing because I'm happy,
I sing because I'm free
For His eye is on the sparrow
And I know He watches me.

II

"Let not your heart be troubled"
His tender words I hear
And resting on His goodness,
I lose my doubt and fear.
Tho' by the path He leadeth
But one step I may see.

III

Whenever I am tempted
Whenever clouds arise
When songs give place to sighing
When hope within me dies
I draw the closer to Him.
From care He sets me free.

She Sherwin

She Sherw

She

Sherwin

sir men whas
mas win resh